Google Certified Professional Cloud Architect A Practical Study Guide to Master the GCP Exam

Introduction

In an era defined by the omnipresence of technology, cloud computing stands as the backbone of innovation, enabling businesses to transcend traditional boundaries and embrace a future where scalability, efficiency, and agility are paramount. At the forefront of this digital revolution is Google Cloud, offering a robust platform that empowers organizations to architect and deploy solutions that are both cutting-edge and resilient.

This book is your indispensable companion on the journey to becoming a certified professional in cloud architecture, particularly within the Google Cloud ecosystem. Whether you're a seasoned IT professional looking to validate your skills or a newcomer eager to dive into the world of cloud computing, this book is tailored to equip you with the knowledge and confidence needed to ace the Google Certified Professional Cloud Architect (GCP-PCA) exam.

In-Depth Coverage of GCP-PCA Exam Domains: Explore the core domains of the Google Certified Professional Cloud Architect exam, delving into topics such as designing and planning, managing and provisioning, implementing security and compliance, optimizing and operating, and ensuring reliability.

Realistic Practice Exam Questions: Enhance your exam readiness with a comprehensive collection of practice questions designed to mimic the format and complexity of the actual GCP-PCA exam. These questions are strategically crafted to challenge your understanding of key concepts and prepare you for the diverse scenarios you may encounter during the test.

Detailed Explanations and Solutions: Every practice question comes with detailed explanations and solutions, providing invaluable insights into the reasoning behind each answer. This not only aids in reinforcing your understanding but also helps you identify and address any knowledge gaps.

Strategic Exam-Taking Tips: Benefit from expert advice on effective exam strategies, time management, and how to approach different types of questions. These tips are designed to boost your confidence and optimize your performance on exam day.

Real-World Case Studies: Learn from real-world case studies that illustrate how Google Cloud solutions have been successfully implemented in various industries. This practical approach allows you to connect theoretical knowledge with practical applications, enhancing your ability to design effective cloud architectures.

By the time you finish reading this guide you will not only possess the skills required to pass the GCP-PCA exam but also be well-equipped to tackle real-world challenges as a certified professional cloud architect. Embark on this transformative journey, and let's navigate the clouds together!

Chapter 1: Introduction to the Professional Cloud Architect Certification

The Google Certified Professional Cloud Architect (GCP-PCA) certification stands as a testament to an individual's expertise in designing, implementing, and managing solutions on Google Cloud Platform (GCP). In this chapter, we will explore the significance of this certification, reasons to pursue it, and provide essential tips on how to navigate the journey towards becoming a Professional Cloud Architect.

Significance of the GCP-PCA Certification

In a world increasingly reliant on cloud solutions, the role of a Professional Cloud Architect has become pivotal. This certification from Google Cloud validates the skills and knowledge required to create scalable and reliable cloud architecture. Professionals with GCP-PCA certification are recognized for their ability to design and optimize GCP solutions, making them highly sought-after in the tech industry.

Reasons to Take the Professional Cloud Architect Exam

Industry Recognition and Credibility:

The GCP-PCA certification is widely acknowledged in the industry, signifying a professional's competence in cloud architecture.

It serves as a powerful differentiator, distinguishing certified individuals as experts in designing robust and scalable cloud solutions.

Career Advancement:

The demand for cloud architects is on the rise, and holding the GCP-PCA certification opens doors to exciting career opportunities.

Many organizations prioritize hiring certified professionals, making it a valuable asset for career growth.

Hands-on Experience with Google Cloud Platform:

The certification process involves practical knowledge and application of GCP services, ensuring that certified individuals have hands-on experience with the platform.

Staying Current in a Dynamic Field:

Google Cloud Platform is continuously evolving, and the certification process requires candidates to stay updated with the latest advancements.

Holding the GCP-PCA certification demonstrates an individual's commitment to continuous learning and staying relevant in a dynamic field.

General Tips on Taking Technical Certification Exams

Preparing for a technical certification exam requires a strategic approach to ensure success. Here are some general tips that can be applied to the GCP-PCA certification and other technical exams:

Understand the Exam Objectives:

Review the official exam guide to understand the domains and topics covered in the certification. This provides a roadmap for your study plan.

Create a Study Plan:

Develop a comprehensive study plan that allocates sufficient time to each exam domain. Consider your existing knowledge and focus on areas where you need improvement.

Utilize Official Documentation and Resources:

Google Cloud provides extensive documentation and resources. Make sure to leverage official documentation, whitepapers, and case studies to deepen your understanding of GCP services.

Hands-on Practice:

Theoretical knowledge is essential, but hands-on experience is equally crucial. Set up a GCP account and actively engage with the platform to reinforce your learning.

Join Communities and Forums:

Participate in online forums and communities dedicated to cloud architecture. Engage with other professionals, ask questions, and share your knowledge to gain diverse perspectives.

Take Practice Exams:

Practice exams are invaluable for assessing your readiness. Identify areas where you struggle and revisit the relevant topics for reinforcement.

Time Management During the Exam:

During the actual exam, manage your time wisely. Allocate specific time slots for each question, and if unsure about an answer, mark it for review and move on to the next.

How to Use the Supplementary Resources

To enhance your preparation for the GCP-PCA exam, it's essential to leverage supplementary resources effectively. These resources complement the official documentation and study materials, providing a well-rounded learning experience.

Online Courses and Tutorials:

Explore online courses and tutorials offered by reputable platforms. These resources often provide in-depth explanations, practical examples, and hands-on labs to reinforce your understanding.

Books and Study Guides:

Utilize books and study guides specifically designed for the GCP-PCA exam. Look for materials that cover the exam objectives comprehensively and include practice questions for self-assessment.

Video Lectures and Webinars:

Video lectures and webinars offer a dynamic way to learn complex concepts. Platforms like YouTube, Coursera, and Google Cloud's official channels host a variety of video content related to cloud architecture.

Mock Exams and Practice Questions:

Take advantage of mock exams and practice questions from different sources. These resources simulate the exam environment, helping you familiarize yourself with the question format and assess your readiness.

Community Study Groups:

Join or form study groups with fellow exam candidates. Collaborative learning can provide diverse insights, clarification of doubts, and a supportive environment for exam preparation.

Interactive Labs and Sandboxes:

Some platforms offer interactive labs and sandboxes that allow you to experiment with GCP services in a risk-free environment. Engaging with these hands-on activities reinforces practical skills.

Embarking on the journey to become a Google Certified Professional Cloud Architect requires a combination of theoretical knowledge, hands-on experience, and strategic preparation. By understanding the significance of the certification, following general tips for exam success, and effectively using supplementary resources, you can position yourself for success in the dynamic field of cloud architecture.

Practice Exam Questions and Answers:

Question 1:

To optimize the performance of your Google Cloud Storage, which storage class is suitable for frequently accessed data that requires low latency and high throughput?

A. Standard Storage Class

B. Nearline Storage Class

C. Coldline Storage Class

D. Archive Storage Class

Correct Answer: A

Feedback:

The Standard Storage Class is designed for frequently accessed data that requires low latency and high throughput, making it suitable for optimizing performance.

Question 2:

When designing a highly available and fault-tolerant application architecture on Google Cloud, which load balancing option provides global load balancing with a single IP address for clients worldwide?

A. Regional Load Balancer

B. Network Load Balancer

C. Internal Load Balancer

D. Global Load Balancer

Correct Answer: D

Feedback:

The Global Load Balancer provides global load balancing with a single IP address for clients worldwide, ensuring high availability and fault tolerance across multiple regions.

Question 3:

To secure communication between services within a Google Kubernetes Engine (GKE) cluster, what is the recommended approach?

A. Use unencrypted communication for faster performance.

B. Implement Network Policies to control traffic between pods.

C. Rely on default security settings provided by GKE.

D. Disable RBAC (Role-Based Access Control) for simplicity.

Correct Answer: B

Feedback:

Implementing Network Policies is the recommended approach to secure communication between services within a GKE cluster. Network Policies allow you to control and define the communication rules between pods.

Question 4:

When deploying applications on Google App Engine, which scaling type allows the application to automatically adjust the number of instances based on incoming traffic?

A. Manual Scaling

B. Basic Scaling

C. Automatic Scaling

D. Dynamic Scaling

Correct Answer: C

Feedback:

Automatic Scaling in Google App Engine allows the application to automatically adjust the number of instances based on incoming traffic, ensuring optimal performance and resource utilization.

Question 5:

To enhance the security of data stored in Google Cloud Storage, what encryption option should you choose?

A. No Encryption

B. Client-Side Encryption

C. Server-Side Encryption with Customer-Managed Keys (CMEK)

D. Server-Side Encryption with Google-Managed Keys (GMEK)

Correct Answer: C and D

Feedback:

Both Server-Side Encryption with Customer-Managed Keys (CMEK) and Server-Side Encryption with Google-Managed Keys (GMEK) enhance the security of data stored in Google Cloud Storage. CMEK allows you to manage your encryption keys, while GMEK uses keys managed by Google.

Question 6:

When setting up a Cloud Identity and Access Management (IAM) policy, what role should you assign to grant full access to all resources within a Google Cloud project?

A. Editor

B. Viewer

C. Owner

D. Administrator

Correct Answer: C

Feedback:

The Owner role in Cloud IAM grants full access to all resources within a Google Cloud project, providing complete control over the project's configuration and resources.

Question 7:

To optimize costs and ensure efficient resource usage in Google Cloud, what feature can you use to automatically shut down instances during non-business hours and weekends?

A. Scheduled Snapshots

B. Auto Scaling

C. Preemptible Instances

D. Instance Templates

Correct Answer: B

Feedback

Auto Scaling allows you to automatically adjust the number of instances based on predefined criteria, including shutting down instances during non-business hours and weekends to optimize costs.

Question 8:

When designing a Google Cloud Platform (GCP) solution for high availability, which networking option provides redundancy at the IP level across multiple regions?

A. VPC Peering

B. VPN (Virtual Private Network)

C. Cloud Router

D. Anycast IP Addressing

Correct Answer: D

Feedback:

Anycast IP Addressing provides redundancy at the IP level across multiple regions, enhancing high availability in a Google Cloud Platform solution.

Question 9:

To ensure data integrity and consistency in Cloud Spanner, what is the recommended isolation level for transactions?

A. Read Committed

B. Repeatable Read

C. Serializable

D. Snapshot Isolation

Correct Answer: C

Feedback:

Serializable is the recommended isolation level for transactions in Cloud Spanner to ensure the highest level of data integrity and consistency.

Question 10:

When configuring a firewall rule in Google Cloud, what is the correct approach to allow incoming traffic only from a specific IP address range?

A. Allow traffic from 0.0.0.0/0 (Any IP)

B. Allow traffic from 127.0.0.1 (Localhost)

C. Allow traffic from the specific IP address range

D. Allow traffic from all IP addresses by default

Correct Answer: C

Feedback:

To allow incoming traffic only from a specific IP address range, configure the firewall rule to explicitly allow traffic from that range, enhancing security by restricting access.

Question 11:

In a Google Kubernetes Engine (GKE) cluster, what is the purpose of a Pod?

A. To provide storage for data persistence.

B. To manage network routing between services.

C. To define the desired state for the deployment.

D. To encapsulate a set of containers with shared storage.

Correct Answer: D

Feedback:

A Pod in GKE encapsulates a set of containers with shared storage and network resources, allowing them to work together as a single unit.

Question 12:

When optimizing the performance of a Google Cloud SQL database, what caching mechanism can you use to reduce the latency of frequently accessed data?

A. Object Storage Caching

B. In-Memory Caching

C. Disk-Based Caching

D. External Caching

Correct Answer: B

Feedback:

In-Memory Caching is a caching mechanism that can be used to reduce the latency of frequently accessed data in a Google Cloud SQL database, as it stores data in memory for faster retrieval.

Question 13:

To improve the reliability of a Google Cloud Function, what should you implement to ensure that the function is retried in case of a transient error?

A. Retry Logic in the Function Code

B. Scheduled Execution

C. Event Trigger Monitoring

D. Cloud Monitoring Alerts

Correct Answer: A

Feedback

Implementing Retry Logic in the Function Code allows for automatic retries in case of transient errors, improving the reliability of a Google Cloud Function.

Question 14:

When deploying a web application on Google App Engine, which authentication method is recommended to secure access to the application?

A. Username and Password Authentication

B. API Key Authentication

C. OAuth 2.0 Authentication

D. IP-Based Authentication

Correct Answer: C

Feedback:

OAuth 2.0 Authentication is the recommended method to secure access to a web application deployed on Google App Engine, providing secure and standardized user authentication.

Question 15:

In Cloud Storage, what is the primary purpose of a bucket?

A. To organize files into directories.

B. To define access control policies.

C. To store data objects and files.

D. To manage lifecycle policies for objects.

Correct Answer: C

Feedback:

The primary purpose of a bucket in Cloud Storage is to store data objects and files, providing a container for organizing and managing stored data.

Question 16:

To improve the security of data in transit between a user's browser and a web application hosted on Google Cloud, what should you implement?

A. IP Whitelisting

B. HTTPS (HTTP Secure)

C. Token-Based Authentication

D. HMAC (Hash-Based Message Authentication Code)

Correct Answer: B

Feedback:

Implementing HTTPS (HTTP Secure) improves the security of data in transit between a user's browser and a web application hosted on Google Cloud by encrypting the communication.

Question 17:

When configuring a Google Cloud Load Balancer, what is the purpose of the health check?

A. To determine the geographic location of the client.

B. To monitor the status and health of backend instances.

C. To define the routing rules for incoming traffic.

D. To perform load balancing based on round-robin distribution.

Correct Answer: B

Feedback:

The health check in a Google Cloud Load Balancer is used to monitor the status and health of backend instances, ensuring that traffic is directed to healthy instances.

Question 18:

In a Google Cloud Pub/Sub architecture, what role is responsible for creating and managing topics and subscriptions?

A. Publisher

B. Subscriber

C. Admin

D. Editor

Correct Answer: C

Feedback:

The Admin role in Google Cloud Pub/Sub is responsible for creating and managing topics and subscriptions, controlling access to the messaging infrastructure.

Question 19:

To enforce access controls and permissions for resources in a Google Cloud project, what service should you use?

A. Cloud Identity

B. Cloud IAM (Identity and Access Management)

C. Cloud Security Command Center

D. Cloud Audit Logging

Correct Answer: B

Feedback:

Cloud IAM (Identity and Access Management) is the service used to enforce access controls and permissions for resources in a Google Cloud project, allowing you to manage and control who can access resources.

Question 20:

When deploying a virtual machine instance on Google Compute Engine, what is the purpose of a custom image?

A. To store user data and configurations.

B. To create a snapshot of the instance's current state.

C. To serve as a template for creating additional instances.

D. To define the instance's network and firewall settings.

Correct Answer: C

Feedback:

A custom image in Google Compute Engine serves as a template for creating additional instances, allowing you to replicate configurations and settings easily.

Question 21:

In Cloud Spanner, what is the purpose of the TrueTime API?

A. To measure the latency of queries.

B. To synchronize clocks across instances.

C. To enforce transaction isolation.

D. To generate unique identifiers for data.

Correct Answer: B

Feedback:

The TrueTime API in Cloud Spanner is used to synchronize clocks across instances, ensuring accurate and consistent timekeeping for transactions.

Question 22:

To improve the reliability of a Google Cloud Storage bucket, what should you implement to automatically replicate data to multiple locations?

A. Object Versioning

B. Object Lifecycle Management

C. Object Change Notifications

D. Object Location Policy

Correct Answer: A

Feedback:

Object Versioning in Google Cloud Storage allows you to automatically replicate data to multiple locations, improving the reliability of the bucket by providing redundancy.

Question 23:

When designing a solution for real-time analytics on Google Cloud, what service can you use to process streaming data and generate real-time insights?

A. Cloud Dataflow

B. BigQuery

C. Cloud Dataprep

D. Cloud Dataproc

Correct Answer: A and B

Feedback:

Both Cloud Dataflow and BigQuery can be used for real-time analytics on Google Cloud. Cloud Dataflow processes streaming data, while BigQuery enables real-time querying and analysis of large datasets.

Question 24:

In Cloud Storage, what is the primary purpose of a signed URL?

A. To provide public access to a file.

B. To encrypt data before storing it.

C. To grant temporary and secure access to private files.

D. To define access control policies for a bucket.

Correct Answer: C

Feedback:

A signed URL in Cloud Storage is used to grant temporary and secure access to private files, providing controlled and time-limited access to resources.

Question 25:

When implementing a CI/CD (Continuous Integration/Continuous Deployment) pipeline on Google Cloud, what service can you use to automate the building and testing of your application?

A. Cloud Build

B. Cloud Composer

C. Cloud Deployment Manager

D. Cloud Source Repositories

Correct Answer: A

Feedback:

Cloud Build in Google Cloud is the service used to automate the building and testing of applications in a CI/CD pipeline, providing a streamlined and automated development process.

Question 26:

In a Google Kubernetes Engine (GKE) cluster, what is the purpose of a Deployment?

A. To manage network traffic routing between services.

B. To define the desired state for a set of pods.

C. To allocate persistent storage to containers.

D. To encapsulate a set of containers with shared resources.

Correct Answer: B

Feedback:

A Deployment in GKE is used to define the desired state for a set of pods, ensuring that the specified number of replicas is running and managing updates to the application.

Question 27:

To optimize costs when using Google Cloud Bigtable, what is the recommended approach for data storage?

A. Use SSD (Solid State Drive) storage for all data.

B. Store data with infrequent access in a Coldline Storage Class.

C. Enable data compression for all tables.

D. Use a single-node cluster to minimize costs.

Correct Answer: C

Feedback

Enabling data compression for tables in Google Cloud Bigtable is the recommended approach to optimize costs, as it reduces storage space and enhances performance.

Question 28:

When designing a Google Cloud Platform (GCP) solution for disaster recovery, what is the purpose of a multi-region deployment?

A. To distribute traffic evenly across multiple regions.

B. To replicate data across multiple regions for redundancy.

C. To allocate resources in different geographic locations.

D. To synchronize clocks for accurate timestamping.

Correct Answer: B

Feedback:

A multi-region deployment in GCP is used to replicate data across multiple regions for redundancy, enhancing disaster recovery capabilities by providing backup locations.

Question 29:

To secure access to a Google Cloud Function, what authentication mechanism is recommended for authorizing HTTP requests?

A. API Key Authentication

B. OAuth 2.0 Authentication

C. HMAC (Hash-Based Message Authentication Code)

D. Identity-Aware Proxy (IAP)

Correct Answer: D

Feedback:

Identity-Aware Proxy (IAP) is the recommended authentication mechanism for securing access to a Google Cloud Function by authorizing HTTP requests, providing centralized and identity-based access control.

Question 30:

In Cloud Spanner, what is the purpose of the Commit Timestamp?

A. To timestamp when a transaction is started.

B. To timestamp when a transaction is committed.

C. To timestamp when a transaction is rolled back.

D. To timestamp when a transaction is read.

Correct Answer: B

Feedback:

The Commit Timestamp in Cloud Spanner is used to timestamp when a transaction is committed, providing a globally ordered and unique timestamp for committed data.

Question 31:

When designing a Google Cloud Platform (GCP) solution for high availability, what load balancing option is suitable for distributing traffic across multiple instances within a single region?

A. Global Load Balancer

B. Regional Load Balancer

C. Internal Load Balancer

D. Network Load Balancer

Correct Answer: B

Feedback:

A Regional Load Balancer in GCP is suitable for distributing traffic across multiple instances within a single region, providing high availability and fault tolerance.

Question 32:

In a Google Kubernetes Engine (GKE) cluster, what is the purpose of a Service?

A. To encapsulate a set of containers with shared storage.

B. To manage network traffic routing between pods.

C. To define the desired state for the deployment.

D. To allocate persistent storage to containers.

Correct Answer: B

Feedback:

A Service in a GKE cluster is used to manage network traffic routing between pods, providing a stable endpoint for accessing the application.

Question 33:

When configuring a Cloud Storage bucket for versioning, what is the impact on storage costs?

A. Versioning has no impact on storage costs.

B. Storage costs increase due to additional metadata.

C. Storage costs decrease for archived versions.

D. Storage costs increase for each versioned object.

Correct Answer: D

Feedback:

Enabling versioning in a Cloud Storage bucket increases storage costs for each versioned object, as each version is stored separately.

Question 34:

To ensure data consistency in a Google Cloud Storage bucket, what storage class is suitable for infrequently accessed data with low retrieval requirements?

A. Standard Storage Class

B. Nearline Storage Class

C. Coldline Storage Class

D. Archive Storage Class

Correct Answer: C

Feedback:

The Coldline Storage Class in Cloud Storage is suitable for infrequently accessed data with low retrieval requirements, providing cost-effective storage with a slightly longer retrieval time.

Question 35:

In Google Cloud Identity and Access Management (IAM), what is the purpose of a Service Account?

A. To represent a Google Cloud user.

B. To define access control policies for resources.

C. To authenticate and authorize applications and services.

D. To manage billing and subscription information.

Correct Answer: C

Feedback:

A Service Account in Google Cloud IAM is used to authenticate and authorize applications and services, providing secure access to resources without the need for user credentials.

Question 36:

When configuring a Google Cloud Load Balancer, what is the purpose of the backend service?

A. To define the routing rules for incoming traffic.

B. To monitor the status and health of backend instances.

C. To perform load balancing based on round-robin distribution.

D. To distribute traffic to backend instances based on defined criteria.

Correct Answer: D

Feedback:

The backend service in a Google Cloud Load Balancer is used to distribute traffic to backend instances based on defined criteria, ensuring efficient load balancing.

Question 37:

To optimize costs when using Google Cloud Dataprep, what is the recommended approach for managing the processing of large datasets?

A. Use a single-node cluster for simplicity.

B. Increase the number of nodes in the cluster.

C. Use preemptible instances for cost-effective processing.

D. Store intermediate data in a Cloud Storage bucket.

Correct Answer: C

Feedback:

Using preemptible instances in a Google Cloud Dataprep cluster is the recommended approach for cost-effective processing of large datasets, as preemptible instances provide significant cost savings.

Question 38:

When designing a Google Cloud Platform (GCP) solution for data residency, what is the purpose of a region?

A. To distribute traffic evenly across multiple regions.

B. To replicate data across multiple regions for redundancy.

C. To specify the geographic location of resources.

D. To synchronize clocks for accurate timestamping.

Correct Answer: C

Feedback:

A region in GCP is used to specify the geographic location of resources, allowing you to control where your data is stored for compliance with data residency requirements.

Question 39:

To enhance the security of a Google Kubernetes Engine (GKE) cluster, what should you implement to control which IP addresses can access the cluster's API server?

A. Network Policies

B. Ingress Controllers

C. Role-Based Access Control (RBAC)

D. Pod Security Policies

Correct Answer: A

Feedback:

Implementing Network Policies in a GKE cluster is the recommended approach to control which IP addresses can access the cluster's API server, enhancing security by defining communication rules between pods.

Chapter 2: Overview of Cloud Computing and Google Cloud

Cloud computing has emerged as a transformative force, reshaping the landscape of technology and offering unparalleled advantages in terms of scalability, flexibility, and efficiency. In this chapter, we will delve into the fundamental concepts of cloud computing and then focus specifically on Google Cloud, exploring its unique features and capabilities.

Overview of Cloud Computing

Cloud computing is a paradigm that involves delivering computing services over the internet, allowing users to access resources and applications without the need for on-premises infrastructure. This model is characterized by on-demand availability, scalability, and pay-as-you-go pricing, making it an attractive solution for businesses of all sizes.

One of the key benefits of cloud computing is the ability to offload the burden of hardware management and maintenance, enabling organizations to focus on their core competencies. Services in the cloud are typically categorized into three main models: Infrastructure as a Service (IaaS), Platform as a Service (PaaS), and Software as a Service (SaaS).

IaaS provides virtualized computing resources, such as virtual machines and storage, allowing users to build and manage their own applications.

PaaS offers a platform with tools and services for application development, abstracting the complexities of infrastructure management.

SaaS delivers fully functional software applications over the internet, eliminating the need for users to install, maintain, and update software locally.

Google Cloud vs. Other Clouds

Security First

Google Cloud is renowned for its robust security measures, implementing a defense-in-depth strategy that spans the entire infrastructure. This includes encryption in transit and at rest, identity and access management controls, and continuous monitoring for potential threats. Google Cloud's security posture is designed to instill confidence in users, ensuring the protection of their data and applications.

Open Cloud

Google Cloud advocates for an open cloud ecosystem, promoting interoperability and preventing vendor lock-in. It supports a wide range of programming languages, frameworks, and operating systems, allowing users to choose the tools that best align with their needs. This commitment to openness fosters innovation and flexibility in application development and deployment.

Analytics and Artificial Intelligence

A standout feature of Google Cloud is its emphasis on analytics and artificial intelligence (AI). The platform offers a suite of tools for data analytics, machine learning, and AI, empowering users to extract valuable insights from their data. From BigQuery for data warehousing to TensorFlow for machine learning, Google Cloud provides a comprehensive set of tools for data-driven decision-making.

Global Data Centers and Network

Google Cloud's global infrastructure spans multiple data centers strategically located around the world. This global footprint ensures low-latency access to services and enables redundancy for increased reliability. The platform's robust and high-performance network connects these data centers, facilitating seamless communication and data transfer.

Principles of System Design

Google Cloud adheres to principles of system design that prioritize reliability, scalability, and maintainability. Services are designed with redundancy and failover mechanisms, ensuring continuous availability even in the face of hardware failures. Scalability is achieved through horizontal scaling, allowing applications to handle increased workloads by adding more resources.

A 10,000-foot Overview of GCP

Google Cloud Platform (GCP) is a comprehensive suite of cloud services that encompasses a wide range of solutions for diverse business needs. Let's take a closer look at the key offerings within GCP.

Computer Solutions

GCP's compute solutions provide the foundation for running applications and services. Compute Engine offers virtual machines with customizable configurations, while Kubernetes Engine facilitates containerized application deployment and management. These services cater to different application architectures, from traditional monoliths to modern microservices.

Storage Solutions

GCP's storage solutions cater to the diverse needs of storing and retrieving data. Cloud Storage offers scalable and durable object storage, suitable for a variety of use cases. Cloud Filestore provides a fully managed file storage service, and Cloud SQL offers managed relational databases for applications that require structured data storage.

Database Solutions

GCP's database solutions cover a spectrum of requirements, from traditional relational databases to NoSQL and fully managed databases. Cloud Spanner, for instance, is a globally distributed, horizontally scalable database, while Firestore is a NoSQL document database designed for web, mobile, and server applications.

Data Analytics

GCP's data analytics services enable organizations to derive insights from their data. BigQuery, a serverless, highly scalable data warehouse, allows for fast SQL queries on large datasets. Dataflow facilitates real-time and batch processing of data, while Dataprep offers intelligent data preparation.

Networking Solutions

Networking is a crucial aspect of any cloud platform, and GCP provides a range of networking solutions. Virtual Private Cloud (VPC) allows users to create isolated network environments, while Cloud Load Balancing ensures high availability and reliability for applications. Cloud CDN (Content Delivery Network) optimizes the delivery of web content to users globally.

Operations Solutions

GCP's operations solutions focus on monitoring, logging, and managing the performance of applications and infrastructure. Stackdriver provides a suite of tools for monitoring, logging, and diagnostics, while Operations Suite offers a comprehensive solution for managing and analyzing performance data.

Developer Tools

Facilitating the development and deployment of applications, GCP's developer tools include Cloud Build for continuous integration and continuous delivery (CI/CD) and Cloud Source Repositories for version control. These tools streamline the development lifecycle and enhance collaboration among development teams.

Hybrid Cloud and Multi-Cloud Solutions

Recognizing the importance of hybrid and multi-cloud scenarios, GCP provides solutions for seamlessly integrating on-premises environments with the cloud. Anthos, for instance, allows for application modernization and management across hybrid and multi-cloud environments.

Migration Solutions

GCP offers tools and services to simplify the migration of applications and workloads to the cloud. CloudEndure facilitates the migration of virtual machines, and Transfer Appliance allows for the secure transfer of large volumes of data to GCP.

Security and Identity Solutions

Security is a top priority for GCP, and the platform offers a range of tools for securing applications and data. Identity and Access Management (IAM) controls access to resources, while Cloud Identity-Aware Proxy (IAP) provides an additional layer of security for applications.

Interacting with the GCP

Understanding how to interact with GCP is crucial for effective utilization. The platform provides two primary interfaces: the Google Cloud Console and the Command-Line Interface (CLI). The Console offers a web-based graphical user interface for managing GCP resources, while the CLI allows for programmatic interaction through commands.

Google Cloud Console

The Google Cloud Console is a user-friendly web interface that allows users to manage and monitor their GCP resources. It provides a visual representation of resources, enabling users to navigate through different services, configure settings, and monitor performance. The Console is an excellent starting point for those who prefer a graphical interface.

Command-Line Interface

For users who prefer automation and programmatic interaction, the Command-Line Interface (CLI) is a powerful tool. The CLI allows users to perform various tasks, such as creating and managing resources, through a series of commands. This approach is particularly beneficial for automating repetitive tasks and integrating GCP with other tools and systems.

Business and Technical Context for the Google Cloud Architect

Before delving into the intricacies of Google Cloud, it is essential to establish the context in which a Google Cloud Architect operates. This involves assessing both business and technical requirements to ensure that the solutions implemented align with the overarching goals of the organization.

Assessing Business Requirements

Business requirements form the foundation upon which technical solutions are built. Google Cloud Architects need to collaborate closely with stakeholders to understand the objectives, challenges, and opportunities within the organization. This involves identifying key business drivers, such as cost optimization, scalability, and innovation, and aligning them with the capabilities of Google Cloud.

Furthermore, considerations like compliance, security, and industry-specific regulations must be taken into account. By thoroughly understanding the business context, Google Cloud Architects can design solutions that not only meet current needs but also position the organization for future success.

Assessing Technical Requirements

In tandem with business requirements, the technical landscape must be thoroughly assessed. This involves evaluating existing infrastructure, applications, and data to identify areas that can benefit from cloud solutions. Considerations include the compatibility of current systems with cloud services, the need for data migration, and the impact on existing workflows.

A comprehensive analysis of technical requirements allows Google Cloud Architects to make informed decisions about the architecture, selecting the most suitable GCP services to meet the organization's goals. Factors such as performance, reliability, and scalability play a crucial role in shaping the technical blueprint.

In conclusion, this chapter provides a foundational understanding of cloud computing, introduces the distinctive features of Google Cloud, and outlines the key services within the Google Cloud Platform. As we progress through this guide, we will delve deeper into each aspect, equipping you with the knowledge and skills necessary to navigate the complexities of the Google Certified Professional Cloud Architect exam and excel in architecting solutions on the Google Cloud Platform.

Practice Exam Questions and Answers:

Q No. 1: What is the purpose of Cloud Identity and Access Management (IAM) in Google Cloud?

A. It allows you to access your Gmail account securely.

B. It helps you manage and control access to Google Cloud resources.

C. It provides email services for your cloud applications.

D. It is a tool for managing virtual machines in Google Cloud.

Correct Answer: B

Feedback:

IAM in Google Cloud is designed to manage and control access to resources. It enables you to grant specific permissions to users, allowing them to interact with Google Cloud resources securely. Options A, C, and D are incorrect because they misrepresent the primary purpose of IAM.

Q No. 2: In Google Cloud, what is the purpose of Cloud Storage?

A. To create virtual machines.

B. To store and retrieve objects, such as files and images.

C. To manage and provision network resources.

D. To analyze large datasets using SQL queries.

Correct Answer: B

Feedback:

Cloud Storage in Google Cloud is a scalable object storage solution used for storing and retrieving objects such as files and images. Options A, C, and D describe functions associated with other Google Cloud services, not Cloud Storage.

Q No. 3: When designing a cloud architecture, what does the term "high availability" refer to?

A. Ensuring that services are available only during business hours.

B. Maximizing uptime and minimizing downtime for applications and services.

C. Limiting access to resources based on user roles.

D. Storing data redundantly to prevent data loss.

Correct Answer: B

Feedback:

High availability in cloud architecture refers to maximizing uptime and minimizing downtime for applications and services. It ensures that systems are accessible and operational for an extended period. Options A, C, and D are incorrect because they do not accurately represent the concept of high availability.

Q No. 4: What is the primary purpose of a Virtual Private Cloud (VPC) in Google Cloud?

A. To create virtual machines.

B. To provide a private, isolated network within the public cloud.

C. To manage and store large datasets.

D. To distribute content globally using a Content Delivery Network (CDN).

Correct Answer: B

Feedback:

A Virtual Private Cloud (VPC) in Google Cloud is designed to provide a private, isolated network within the public cloud. It allows you to define and control a logically isolated section of the Google Cloud infrastructure. Options A, C, and D describe functionalities associated with other Google Cloud services.

Q No. 5: What is the purpose of Cloud Spanner in Google Cloud?

A. To provide a fully managed file storage service.

B. To offer scalable and durable object storage.

C. To facilitate globally distributed, horizontally scalable databases.

D. To perform real-time and batch processing of data.

Correct Answer: C

Feedback:

Cloud Spanner in Google Cloud is a globally distributed, horizontally scalable database. It is designed to provide strong consistency and support for ACID transactions across regions. Options A, B, and D describe functionalities associated with other Google Cloud services, not Cloud Spanner.

Q No. 6: Why is it important to use Cloud Load Balancing in a multi-zone deployment?

A. It reduces the cost of deploying resources in multiple zones.

B. It distributes incoming network traffic evenly across multiple instances in different zones.

C. It ensures that resources are only deployed in a single zone for cost efficiency.

D. It provides additional security by isolating instances in different zones.

Correct Answer: B

Feedback:

Cloud Load Balancing in Google Cloud evenly distributes incoming network traffic across multiple instances in different zones. This enhances the availability and fault tolerance of applications by ensuring that no single zone bears the entire load. Options A, C, and D do not accurately represent the purpose of Cloud Load Balancing.

Q No. 7: What is the significance of horizontal scaling in cloud computing?

A. It involves adding more resources to a single virtual machine.

B. It refers to increasing the capacity of a single server.

C. It enables the addition of more instances to distribute the load across multiple resources.

D. It involves upgrading the hardware of a physical server.

Correct Answer: C

Feedback:

Horizontal scaling in cloud computing involves adding more instances to distribute the load across multiple resources. It allows applications to handle increased workloads by adding more virtual machines or containers. Options A, B, and D describe concepts associated with vertical scaling or hardware upgrades.

Q No. 8: When is it advisable to use Cloud SQL in Google Cloud?

A. For managing and storing large datasets.

B. For globally distributed, horizontally scalable databases.

C. For scalable and durable object storage.

D. For managing relational databases.

Correct Answer: D

Feedback:

Cloud SQL in Google Cloud is designed for managing relational databases. It offers a fully managed, highly available, and secure database service that supports various database engines. Options A, B, and C describe functionalities associated with other Google Cloud services, not Cloud SQL.

Q No. 9: What is the purpose of Cloud Identity-Aware Proxy (IAP) in Google Cloud?

A. To manage and control access to Google Cloud resources.

B. To perform real-time and batch processing of data.

C. To facilitate globally distributed, horizontally scalable databases.

D. To provide an additional layer of security for applications.

Correct Answer: D

Feedback:

Cloud Identity-Aware Proxy (IAP) in Google Cloud provides an additional layer of security for applications. It verifies the identity of users and checks for their authorization before allowing access to applications. Options A, B, and C describe functionalities associated with other Google Cloud services.

Q No. 10: How does Google Cloud promote interoperability and prevent vendor lock-in?

A. By supporting a wide range of programming languages, frameworks, and operating systems.

B. By restricting access to resources based on user roles.

C. By providing email services for cloud applications.

D. By creating virtual machines with customizable configurations.

Correct Answer: A

Feedback:

Google Cloud promotes interoperability and prevents vendor lock-in by supporting a wide range of programming languages, frameworks, and operating systems. This allows users to choose tools that best align with their needs, fostering innovation and flexibility. Options B, C, and D do not accurately represent Google Cloud's approach to interoperability.

Q No. 11: Why is it recommended to use Cloud Endpoints in a microservices architecture?

A. To create virtual machines.

B. To provide a private, isolated network within the public cloud.

C. To facilitate communication and management of APIs in a scalable manner.

D. To perform real-time and batch processing of data.

Correct Answer: C

Feedback:

Cloud Endpoints in Google Cloud is designed to facilitate communication and management of APIs in a scalable manner, especially in a microservices architecture. It provides features like authentication, monitoring, and security for APIs. Options A, B, and D describe functionalities associated with other Google Cloud services, not Cloud Endpoints.

Q No. 12: What is the purpose of Google Cloud's Dataflow service?

A. To provide scalable and durable object storage.

B. To perform real-time and batch processing of data.

C. To create virtual machines with customizable configurations.

D. To offer a fully managed file storage service.

Correct Answer: B

Feedback:

Google Cloud Dataflow is designed for real-time and batch processing of data. It allows you to design and deploy data processing pipelines for tasks like ETL (Extract, Transform, Load) and stream processing. Options A, C, and D describe functionalities associated with other Google Cloud services.

Q No. 13: How does Cloud CDN optimize content delivery in Google Cloud?

A. By providing a private, isolated network within the public cloud.

B. By evenly distributing incoming network traffic across multiple instances.

C. By caching content at strategically located points of presence (PoPs) around the world.

D. By creating virtual machines with customizable configurations.

Correct Answer: C

Feedback:

Cloud CDN in Google Cloud optimizes content delivery by caching content at strategically located points of presence (PoPs) around the world. This reduces latency and improves the performance of delivering web content to users. Options A, B, and D describe functionalities associated with other Google Cloud services.

Q No. 14: In the context of Google Cloud, what is the purpose of Anthos?

A. To provide a private, isolated network within the public cloud.

B. To enable application modernization and management across hybrid and multi-cloud environments.

C. To offer a fully managed file storage service.

D. To facilitate communication and management of APIs in a scalable manner.

Correct Answer: B

Feedback:

Anthos in Google Cloud is designed to enable application modernization and management across hybrid and multi-cloud environments. It allows organizations to build and deploy applications consistently across different environments. Options A, C, and D describe functionalities associated with other Google Cloud services.

Q No. 15: How does Cloud Storage Nearline differ from Cloud Storage Standard in Google Cloud?

A. Cloud Storage Nearline is designed for scalable object storage, while Cloud Storage Standard is for relational databases.

B. Cloud Storage Nearline is suitable for infrequently accessed data with a retrieval time measured in seconds, while Cloud Storage Standard provides low-latency access to frequently accessed data.

C. Cloud Storage Nearline offers fully managed file storage, while Cloud Storage Standard facilitates real-time and batch processing of data.

D. Cloud Storage Nearline is focused on creating virtual machines, while Cloud Storage Standard is for managing and storing large datasets.

Correct Answer: B

Feedback:

Cloud Storage Nearline in Google Cloud is suitable for infrequently accessed data with a retrieval time measured in seconds, while Cloud Storage Standard provides low-latency access to frequently accessed data. Options A, C, and D describe functionalities associated with other Google Cloud services.

Q No. 16: Why is it recommended to use Cloud Monitoring in Google Cloud?

A. To provide a private, isolated network within the public cloud.

B. To enable application modernization and management across hybrid and multi-cloud environments.

C. To manage and control access to Google Cloud resources.

D. To monitor and analyze the performance of applications and infrastructure.

Correct Answer: D

Feedback:

Cloud Monitoring in Google Cloud is recommended to monitor and analyze the performance of applications and infrastructure. It provides insights into the health, performance, and availability of applications and resources. Options A, B, and C describe functionalities associated with other Google Cloud services.

Q No. 17: What is the purpose of Cloud Armor in Google Cloud?

A. To perform real-time and batch processing of data.

B. To provide a private, isolated network within the public cloud.

C. To manage and store large datasets.

D. To protect applications and services from Distributed Denial of Service (DDoS) attacks.

Correct Answer: D

Feedback:

Cloud Armor in Google Cloud is designed to protect applications and services from Distributed Denial of Service (DDoS) attacks. It provides security policies and defenses to safeguard against malicious traffic. Options A, B, and C describe functionalities associated with other Google Cloud services.

Q No. 18: In the context of Google Cloud, what is the purpose of Cloud DNS?

A. To provide scalable and durable object storage.

B. To perform real-time and batch processing of data.

C. To enable application modernization and management across hybrid and multi-cloud environments.

D. To manage and resolve domain names for applications and services.

Correct Answer: D

Feedback:

Cloud DNS in Google Cloud is designed to manage and resolve domain names for applications and services. It provides a reliable and scalable domain name resolution service. Options A, B, and C describe functionalities associated with other Google Cloud services.

Q No. 19: When creating a managed instance group, why is it important to use a health check?

A. To provide a private, isolated network within the public cloud.

B. To monitor and analyze the performance of applications and infrastructure.

C. To enable application modernization and management across hybrid and multi-cloud environments.

D. To ensure that only healthy instances receive traffic.

Correct Answer: D

Feedback:

When creating a managed instance group in Google Cloud, using a health check is important to ensure that only healthy instances receive traffic. Health checks monitor the status of instances and direct traffic away from instances that are not responding correctly. Options A, B, and C describe functionalities associated with other Google Cloud services.

Q No. 20: What is the purpose of Cloud Functions in Google Cloud?

A. To perform real-time and batch processing of data.

B. To enable application modernization and management across hybrid and multi-cloud environments.

C. To create and run serverless functions that respond to events.

D. To provide scalable and durable object storage.

Correct Answer: C

Feedback:

Cloud Functions in Google Cloud is designed to create and run serverless functions that respond to events. It allows developers to execute code in response to various triggers without the need to manage server infrastructure. Options A, B, and D describe functionalities associated with other Google Cloud services.

Chapter 3: Cloud Identity

In the ever-evolving landscape of cloud computing, establishing robust identity and access management (IAM) practices is fundamental to ensuring the security and integrity of digital environments. This chapter delves into the intricate realm of Cloud Identity, covering essential topics such as setting up Cloud Identity and admin accounts, security principles, user management, authentication methods, and security auditing.

Setting Up a Cloud Identity and Admin Account

Introduction:

Creating a foundation for secure and organized cloud operations begins with setting up a Cloud Identity and admin account. Google Cloud provides a comprehensive platform for managing user identities, controlling access to resources, and implementing robust security measures.

Cloud Identity Setup:

Setting up Cloud Identity involves creating a centralized directory for managing users, groups, and devices. This directory serves as the backbone for access management across various Google Cloud services. Administrators can add users, assign roles, and establish policies to govern access.

Admin Account Configuration:

The admin account is the linchpin of Cloud Identity management. Admins wield significant control over the platform, necessitating careful configuration. Best practices include implementing multi-factor authentication (MFA) for admin accounts, enforcing strong password policies, and regularly reviewing and updating permissions.

Security Principles in the Cloud

The AAA Security Model:

Authentication, authorization, and accounting (AAA) constitute the trifecta of security in cloud environments. Authentication verifies the identity of users, authorization dictates what actions they can perform, and accounting maintains a record of these activities. Understanding and implementing the AAA model is critical to building a secure Cloud Identity framework.

Least Privilege and Separation of Duties:

The principles of least privilege and separation of duties are foundational to cloud security. Least privilege ensures that users have the minimum access necessary to perform their roles, reducing the risk of unauthorized actions. Separation of duties further mitigates risks by distributing responsibilities among different users, preventing any single point of failure or malicious activity.

Cloud Identity Overview

Managing Users in Cloud Identity:

User management in Cloud Identity involves creating, modifying, and deactivating user accounts. Administrators can organize users into groups to streamline access control, making it easier to assign permissions to multiple users simultaneously. Proper user management is essential for maintaining an efficient and secure identity infrastructure.

How Users Authenticate to GCP

2-Step Verification:

Two-step verification (2SV) adds an extra layer of security to user authentication. This method requires users to provide two forms of identification: typically a password and a verification code sent to a trusted device. Implementing 2SV enhances the security of Cloud Identity by adding an additional barrier against unauthorized access.

Security Auditing

Introduction to Security Auditing:

Security auditing is the systematic examination of an organization's information systems to identify and assess security-related events. In the context of Cloud Identity, auditing plays a pivotal role in maintaining visibility into user activities, detecting potential security threats, and ensuring compliance with security policies.

Audit Logging in GCP:

Google Cloud Platform (GCP) offers robust audit logging capabilities, allowing organizations to capture detailed records of user activity. This includes changes to IAM policies, access attempts, and administrative actions. Admins can configure audit logs to be stored centrally, enabling efficient monitoring and analysis of security events.

Alerting and Response:

Effective security auditing goes beyond log collection; it involves setting up alerts and responses to potential security incidents. Cloud Identity administrators can leverage

Google Cloud's monitoring and alerting tools to receive real-time notifications of suspicious activities, enabling swift responses to security threats.

Continuous Monitoring and Improvement:

Security is an ongoing process, and auditing is a dynamic component of this process. Continuous monitoring of audit logs allows organizations to adapt to evolving security landscapes. Regularly reviewing and refining security policies based on audit findings ensures that Cloud Identity remains resilient against emerging threats.

Cloud Identity is the cornerstone of secure and efficient cloud operations. This chapter has provided a comprehensive exploration of setting up Cloud Identity and admin accounts, understanding security principles, managing users, implementing authentication methods, and conducting security auditing. As organizations increasingly rely on cloud services, a deep understanding of Cloud Identity is imperative for building and maintaining a robust and resilient security posture in the digital realm. The journey through Cloud Identity is a dynamic one, requiring continuous adaptation to emerging threats and evolving best practices.

Practice Exam Questions and Answers

Q No. 1: What is the primary purpose of Cloud Identity in Google Cloud?

A. To provide scalable and durable object storage.

B. To manage and control access to Google Cloud resources.

C. To create virtual machines with customizable configurations.

D. To facilitate communication and management of APIs.

Correct Answer: B

Feedback:

Cloud Identity in Google Cloud is designed to manage and control access to resources. It provides identity services, user management, and access control to ensure secure and organized cloud operations. Options A, C, and D describe functionalities associated with other Google Cloud services.

Q No. 2: Why is multi-factor authentication (MFA) important in Cloud Identity?

A. It simplifies user authentication processes.

B. It adds an extra layer of security by requiring multiple forms of identification.

C. It enables users to create virtual machines with customizable configurations.

D. It improves the performance of applications and infrastructure.

Correct Answer: B

Feedback:

Multi-factor authentication (MFA) in Cloud Identity adds an extra layer of security by requiring multiple forms of identification, typically a password and a verification code. This enhances the security of user authentication processes. Options A, C, and D describe functionalities associated with other Google Cloud services.

Q No. 3: What are the principles of security that emphasize giving users the minimum access necessary to perform their roles?

A. The CIA Security Model

B. Least Privilege and Separation of Duties

C. The AAA Security Model

D. Identity and Access Management (IAM)

Correct Answer: B

Feedback:

The principles of least privilege and separation of duties emphasize giving users the minimum access necessary to perform their roles, reducing the risk of unauthorized actions. Options A, C, and D describe other security concepts and models.

Q No. 4: What does the AAA Security Model stand for in the context of cloud security?

A. Authentication, Authorization, and Auditing

B. Access, Analysis, and Authorization

C. Authorization, Accounting, and Authentication

D. Access, Authentication, and Analysis

Correct Answer: C

Feedback:

The AAA Security Model in the context of cloud security stands for Authorization, Accounting, and Authentication. These three components form the basis of secure cloud operations. Options A, B, and D provide incorrect interpretations of the AAA model.

Q No. 5: How does Cloud DNS contribute to Cloud Identity?

A. By managing and resolving domain names for applications and services.

B. By providing scalable and durable object storage.

C. By facilitating communication and management of APIs.

D. By creating virtual machines with customizable configurations.

Correct Answer: A

Feedback:

Cloud DNS in Google Cloud contributes to Cloud Identity by managing and resolving domain names for applications and services. It provides a reliable and scalable domain name resolution service. Options B, C, and D describe functionalities associated with other Google Cloud services.

Q No. 6: What is the primary purpose of Cloud Armor in Google Cloud?

A. To create and run serverless functions that respond to events.

B. To provide an additional layer of security for applications.

C. To optimize content delivery through a Content Delivery Network (CDN).

D. To manage and store large datasets.

Correct Answer: B

Feedback:

The primary purpose of Cloud Armor in Google Cloud is to provide an additional layer of security for applications. It protects against Distributed Denial of Service (DDoS) attacks and other malicious activities. Options A, C, and D describe functionalities associated with other Google Cloud services.

Q No. 7: Why is auditing important in Cloud Identity?

A. To provide a private, isolated network within the public cloud.

B. To monitor and analyze the performance of applications and infrastructure.

C. To detect potential security threats and ensure compliance.

D. To create virtual machines with customizable configurations.

Correct Answer: C

Feedback:

Auditing in Cloud Identity is important to detect potential security threats and ensure compliance with security policies. It provides a systematic examination of information systems to maintain visibility into user activities. Options A, B, and D describe functionalities associated with other Google Cloud services.

Q No. 8: How does Cloud Endpoints contribute to Cloud Identity?

A. By providing a fully managed file storage service.

B. By creating and running serverless functions that respond to events.

C. By facilitating communication and management of APIs.

D. By optimizing content delivery through a Content Delivery Network (CDN).

Correct Answer: C

Feedback:

Cloud Endpoints in Google Cloud contributes to Cloud Identity by facilitating communication and management of APIs. It allows for the creation, deployment, and management of scalable and secure APIs. Options A, B, and D describe functionalities associated with other Google Cloud services.

Q No. 9: In the context of Google Cloud, what does Cloud SQL primarily offer?

A. To create virtual machines with customizable configurations.

B. To enable application modernization and management across hybrid and multi-cloud environments.

C. To manage relational databases.

D. To perform real-time and batch processing of data.

Correct Answer: C

Feedback:

In the context of Google Cloud, Cloud SQL primarily offers managed relational databases. It provides a fully managed, highly available, and secure database service supporting various database engines. Options A, B, and D describe functionalities associated with other Google Cloud services.

Q No. 10: What is the primary purpose of Cloud Storage Nearline in Google Cloud?

A. To enable application modernization and management across hybrid and multi-cloud environments.

B. To perform real-time and batch processing of data.

C. To provide scalable and durable object storage for infrequently accessed data.

D. To manage and resolve domain names for applications and services.

Correct Answer: C

Feedback:

The primary purpose of Cloud Storage Nearline in Google Cloud is to provide scalable and durable object storage for infrequently accessed data. It offers a cost-effective solution for long-term storage. Options A, B, and D describe functionalities associated with other Google Cloud services.

Q No. 11: What is the primary function of Cloud Spanner in Google Cloud?

A. To manage and control access to Google Cloud resources.

B. To provide scalable and durable object storage.

C. To facilitate globally distributed, horizontally scalable databases.

D. To create and run serverless functions that respond to events.

Correct Answer: C

Feedback:

Cloud Spanner in Google Cloud is designed to facilitate globally distributed, horizontally scalable databases. It provides strong consistency and supports ACID transactions across regions. Options A, B, and D describe functionalities associated with other Google Cloud services.

Q No. 12: Why is it recommended to use Cloud Monitoring in Google Cloud?

A. To optimize content delivery through a Content Delivery Network (CDN).

B. To manage and control access to Google Cloud resources.

C. To monitor and analyze the performance of applications and infrastructure.

D. To perform real-time and batch processing of data.

Correct Answer: C

Feedback:

Cloud Monitoring in Google Cloud is recommended to monitor and analyze the performance of applications and infrastructure. It provides insights into the health, performance, and availability of applications and resources. Options A, B, and D describe functionalities associated with other Google Cloud services.

Q No. 13: What is the primary purpose of Cloud CDN in Google Cloud?

A. To create virtual machines with customizable configurations.

B. To provide an additional layer of security for applications.

C. To optimize content delivery through a Content Delivery Network (CDN).

D. To perform real-time and batch processing of data.

Correct Answer: C

Feedback:

The primary purpose of Cloud CDN in Google Cloud is to optimize content delivery through a Content Delivery Network (CDN). It caches content at strategically located points of presence (PoPs) around the world, reducing latency. Options A, B, and D describe functionalities associated with other Google Cloud services.

Q No. 14: What is the role of Cloud Functions in Google Cloud?

A. To enable application modernization and management across hybrid and multi-cloud environments.

B. To create and run serverless functions that respond to events.

C. To manage and control access to Google Cloud resources.

D. To provide scalable and durable object storage.

Correct Answer: B

Feedback:

Cloud Functions in Google Cloud is designed to create and run serverless functions that respond to events. It allows developers to execute code in response to various triggers without managing server infrastructure. Options A, C, and D describe functionalities associated with other Google Cloud services.

Q No. 15: How does Cloud Storage Standard differ from Cloud Storage Nearline in Google Cloud?

A. Cloud Storage Standard is designed for scalable object storage, while Cloud Storage Nearline is for relational databases.

B. Cloud Storage Standard provides low-latency access to frequently accessed data, while Cloud Storage Nearline is suitable for infrequently accessed data.

C. Cloud Storage Standard offers fully managed file storage, while Cloud Storage Nearline facilitates real-time and batch processing of data.

D. Cloud Storage Standard is focused on creating virtual machines, while Cloud Storage Nearline is for managing and storing large datasets.

Correct Answer: B

Feedback:

Cloud Storage Standard in Google Cloud provides low-latency access to frequently accessed data, while Cloud Storage Nearline is suitable for infrequently accessed data with a retrieval time measured in seconds. Options A, C, and D describe functionalities associated with other Google Cloud services.

Q No. 16: Why is Cloud Identity-Aware Proxy (IAP) important in Google Cloud?

A. To optimize content delivery through a Content Delivery Network (CDN).

B. To provide an additional layer of security for applications.

C. To manage and control access to Google Cloud resources.

D. To create virtual machines with customizable configurations.

Correct Answer: B

Feedback:

Cloud Identity-Aware Proxy (IAP) in Google Cloud is important to provide an additional layer of security for applications. It verifies user identity and checks for authorization before granting access. Options A, C, and D describe functionalities associated with other Google Cloud services.

Q No. 17: What is the significance of horizontal scaling in cloud computing?

A. It involves adding more resources to a single virtual machine.

B. It refers to increasing the capacity of a single server.

C. It enables the addition of more instances to distribute the load across multiple resources.

D. It involves upgrading the hardware of a physical server.

Correct Answer: C

Feedback:

Horizontal scaling in cloud computing involves adding more instances to distribute the load across multiple resources. It allows applications to handle increased workloads by adding more virtual machines or containers. Options A, B, and D describe concepts associated with vertical scaling or hardware upgrades.

Q No. 18: When is it advisable to use Cloud SQL in Google Cloud?

A. For managing and storing large datasets.

B. For globally distributed, horizontally scalable databases.

C. For scalable and durable object storage.

D. For managing relational databases.

Correct Answer: D

Feedback:

Cloud SQL in Google Cloud is advisable for managing relational databases. It offers a fully managed, highly available, and secure database service supporting various database engines. Options A, B, and C describe functionalities associated with other Google Cloud services.

Q No. 19: What is the purpose of Anthos in the context of Google Cloud?

A. To provide a private, isolated network within the public cloud.

B. To enable application modernization and management across hybrid and multi-cloud environments.

C. To offer a fully managed file storage service.

D. To facilitate communication and management of APIs in a scalable manner.

Correct Answer: B

Feedback:

Anthos in Google Cloud is designed to enable application modernization and management across hybrid and multi-cloud environments. It allows organizations to build and deploy applications consistently across different environments. Options A, C, and D describe functionalities associated with other Google Cloud services.

Q No. 20: How does Cloud Armor contribute to security in Google Cloud?

A. By providing a fully managed file storage service.

B. By creating and running serverless functions that respond to events.

C. By optimizing content delivery through a Content Delivery Network (CDN).

D. By protecting applications and services from Distributed Denial of Service (DDoS) attacks.

Correct Answer: D

Feedback:

Cloud Armor in Google Cloud contributes to security by protecting applications and services from Distributed Denial of Service (DDoS) attacks. It provides security policies and defenses against malicious traffic. Options A, B, and C describe functionalities associated with other Google Cloud services.

Q No. 21 When creating a managed instance group, why is it important to use a health check?

A. To provide a private, isolated network within the public cloud.

B. To monitor and analyze the performance of applications and infrastructure.

C. To enable application modernization and management across hybrid and multi-cloud environments.

D. To ensure that only healthy instances receive traffic.

Correct Answer: D

Feedback:

When creating a managed instance group in Google Cloud, using a health check is important to ensure that only healthy instances receive traffic. Health checks monitor the status of instances and direct traffic away from instances that are not responding correctly. Options A, B, and C describe functionalities associated with other Google Cloud services.

Q No. 22: In the context of Google Cloud, what is the purpose of Cloud DNS?

A. To provide scalable and durable object storage.

B. To perform real-time and batch processing of data.

C. To enable application modernization and management across hybrid and multi-cloud environments.

D. To manage and resolve domain names for applications and services.

Correct Answer: D

Feedback:

Cloud DNS in Google Cloud is designed to manage and resolve domain names for applications and services. It provides a reliable and scalable domain name resolution service. Options A, B, and C describe functionalities associated with other Google Cloud services.

Q No. 23: What is the primary purpose of Google Cloud Dataflow?

A. To create virtual machines with customizable configurations.

B. To perform real-time and batch processing of data.

C. To optimize content delivery through a Content Delivery Network (CDN).

D. To enable application modernization and management across hybrid and multi-cloud environments.

Correct Answer: B

Feedback:

Google Cloud Dataflow is designed for real-time and batch processing of data. It allows you to design and deploy data processing pipelines for tasks like ETL (Extract,

Transform, Load) and stream processing. Options A, C, and D describe functionalities associated with other Google Cloud services.

Q No. 24: How does Cloud Identity contribute to access management in Google Cloud?

A. By managing and resolving domain names for applications and services.

B. By optimizing content delivery through a Content Delivery Network (CDN).

C. By providing identity services, user management, and access control.

D. By creating and running serverless functions that respond to events.

Correct Answer: C

Feedback:

Cloud Identity in Google Cloud contributes to access management by providing identity services, user management, and access control. It establishes a centralized directory for managing users, groups, and devices. Options A, B, and D describe functionalities associated with other Google Cloud services.

Q No. 25: What is the role of Cloud Endpoints in Google Cloud?

A. To provide scalable and durable object storage.

B. To create and run serverless functions that respond to events.

C. To enable application modernization and management across hybrid and multi-cloud environments.

D. To facilitate communication and management of APIs.

Correct Answer: D

Feedback:

Cloud Endpoints in Google Cloud plays a role in facilitating communication and management of APIs. It allows for the creation, deployment, and management of scalable and secure APIs. Options A, B, and C describe functionalities associated with other Google Cloud services.

Q No. 26: What is the purpose of Cloud Identity-Aware Proxy (IAP) in Google Cloud?

A. To manage and control access to Google Cloud resources.

B. To perform real-time and batch processing of data.

C. To enable application modernization and management across hybrid and multi-cloud environments.

D. To provide an additional layer of security for applications.

Correct Answer: D

Feedback:

Cloud Identity-Aware Proxy (IAP) in Google Cloud is designed to provide an additional layer of security for applications. It verifies user identity and checks for authorization before granting access. Options A, B, and C describe functionalities associated with other Google Cloud services.

Q No. 27: How does Cloud CDN optimize content delivery in Google Cloud?

A. By providing a private, isolated network within the public cloud.

B. By evenly distributing incoming network traffic across multiple instances.

C. By caching content at strategically located points of presence (PoPs) around the world.

D. By creating virtual machines with customizable configurations.

Correct Answer: C

Feedback:

Cloud CDN in Google Cloud optimizes content delivery by caching content at strategically located points of presence (PoPs) around the world. This reduces latency and improves the performance of delivering web content to users. Options A, B, and D describe functionalities associated with other Google Cloud services.

Q No. 28: What is the primary purpose of Anthos in Google Cloud?

A. To provide a private, isolated network within the public cloud.

B. To enable application modernization and management across hybrid and multi-cloud environments.

C. To offer a fully managed file storage service.

D. To facilitate communication and management of APIs in a scalable manner.

Correct Answer: B

Feedback:

Anthos in Google Cloud is designed to enable application modernization and management across hybrid and multi-cloud environments. It allows organizations to build and deploy applications consistently across different environments. Options A, C, and D describe functionalities associated with other Google Cloud services.

Q No. 29: How does Cloud Armor contribute to security in Google Cloud?

A. By providing a fully managed file storage service.

B. By creating and running serverless functions that respond to events.

C. By optimizing content delivery through a Content Delivery Network (CDN).

D. By protecting applications and services from Distributed Denial of Service (DDoS) attacks.

Correct Answer: D

Feedback:

Cloud Armor in Google Cloud contributes to security by protecting applications and services from Distributed Denial of Service (DDoS) attacks. It provides security policies and defenses against malicious traffic. Options A, B, and C describe functionalities associated with other Google Cloud services.

Q No. 30: In the context of Google Cloud, what is the purpose of Cloud Storage Nearline?

A. To enable application modernization and management across hybrid and multi-cloud environments.

B. To perform real-time and batch processing of data.

C. To provide scalable and durable object storage for infrequently accessed data.

D. To manage and resolve domain names for applications and services.

Correct Answer: C

Feedback:

In the context of Google Cloud, the purpose of Cloud Storage Nearline is to provide scalable and durable object storage for infrequently accessed data. It offers a cost-effective solution for long-term storage. Options A, B, and D describe functionalities associated with other Google Cloud services.

Chapter 4: Resource Management

In the dynamic landscape of cloud computing, effective resource management is paramount for optimizing performance, ensuring cost efficiency, and maintaining security. This chapter delves into the intricacies of Google Cloud's Resource Manager, providing an overview of its functionalities, the organization hierarchy, and the implementation of organization policies.

Cloud Resource Manager is the foundational service within Google Cloud for organizing and managing resources. It acts as a central hub for creating, organizing, and tracking resources, providing a unified view of an organization's cloud assets. This section explores the core functionalities that empower organizations to streamline resource management.

Cloud Resource Manager offers a range of features, including resource organization, access control, and visibility. It provides a single pane of glass to oversee projects, manage permissions, and track usage. Understanding these features is crucial for effective resource management and optimization.

Organization Hierarchy

The organization hierarchy in Google Cloud consists of interconnected components, each playing a unique role in resource organization and management. This section provides a detailed exploration of the hierarchical structure, comprising organizations, folders, projects, and the resources within.

Organizations:

At the top of the hierarchy is the organization, representing the entire Google Cloud environment for an entity. Understanding the organization is fundamental to establishing a structured and well-organized resource management approach.

Folders:

Folders serve as an organizational unit within an organization, allowing for the logical grouping of projects and resources. They provide a flexible way to structure resources based on departments, teams, or projects, facilitating effective resource management and access control.

Projects:

Projects are the fundamental building blocks within the organization hierarchy. They encapsulate resources and services, defining the scope of billing and permissions. This section elucidates the pivotal role projects play in resource management.

Resources:

Resources within projects encompass a diverse range of cloud services, such as virtual machines, databases, and storage. Effective resource management involves understanding how these resources interact within the organization hierarchy.

Organization Policies

Introduction to Organization Policies:

Organization policies in Google Cloud are a critical tool for enforcing and controlling the behavior of resources. This section provides an in-depth exploration of how organization policies contribute to governance, compliance, and resource management.

Implementation and Best Practices:

Implementing organization policies requires a nuanced understanding of an organization's requirements and regulatory constraints. Best practices for defining, implementing, and managing organization policies are discussed, ensuring a robust and compliant resource management framework.

Use Cases:

Real-world use cases demonstrate the practical applications of organization policies. From enforcing security standards to optimizing resource usage, organization policies play a pivotal role in achieving governance objectives.

Effective resource management in the cloud is a multifaceted endeavor that demands a comprehensive understanding of the tools and structures provided by Google Cloud's Resource Manager. This chapter has provided an overview of the Cloud Resource Manager, elucidated the nuances of the organization hierarchy, and delved into the implementation of organization policies. As organizations navigate the complexities of cloud resource management, mastering these concepts is pivotal for achieving operational excellence, cost efficiency, and security in the cloud.

Practice Exam Questions and Answers

Q No. 1: What is the primary purpose of Google Cloud's Cloud Resource Manager?

A. To provide scalable and durable object storage.

B. To organize and manage cloud resources in a hierarchical structure.

C. To create and run serverless functions that respond to events.

D. To optimize content delivery through a Content Delivery Network (CDN).

Correct Answer: B

Feedback:

Cloud Resource Manager in Google Cloud is designed to organize and manage cloud resources in a hierarchical structure. It acts as a central hub for creating, tracking, and managing resources within an organization.

Q No. 2: In the Google Cloud organization hierarchy, what role does a "Folder" play?

A. It represents an individual user account.

B. It serves as an organizational unit for grouping projects and resources.

C. It encapsulates cloud services such as virtual machines and databases.

D. It is a fundamental building block within a project.

Correct Answer: B

Feedback:

In the Google Cloud organization hierarchy, a "Folder" serves as an organizational unit for grouping projects and resources. It provides a flexible way to structure resources based on departments, teams, or projects.

Q No. 3: What is the purpose of a Google Cloud "Project"?

A. To provide scalable and durable object storage.

B. To represent an individual user account.

C. To encapsulate resources and services, defining the scope of billing and permissions.

D. To optimize content delivery through a Content Delivery Network (CDN).

Correct Answer: C

Feedback:

A Google Cloud "Project" is designed to encapsulate resources and services, defining the scope of billing and permissions within the organization hierarchy.

Q No. 4: How does Cloud Resource Manager contribute to access control in Google Cloud?

A. By optimizing content delivery through a Content Delivery Network (CDN).

B. By providing identity services, user management, and access control.

C. By creating and running serverless functions that respond to events.

D. By managing and resolving domain names for applications and services.

Correct Answer: B

Feedback:

Cloud Resource Manager contributes to access control in Google Cloud by providing identity services, user management, and access control. It establishes a centralized directory for managing users, groups, and devices.

Q No. 5: What is the primary purpose of Google Cloud's Organization Policies?

A. To enable application modernization and management across hybrid and multi-cloud environments.

B. To manage and control access to Google Cloud resources.

C. To create and run serverless functions that respond to events.

D. To enforce and control the behavior of resources within an organization.

Correct Answer: D

Feedback:

The primary purpose of Google Cloud's Organization Policies is to enforce and control the behavior of resources within an organization. They contribute to governance, compliance, and resource management.

Q No. 6: How does a Google Cloud "Folder" contribute to effective resource management?

A. By facilitating communication and management of APIs.

B. By serving as an organizational unit for grouping projects and resources.

C. By providing scalable and durable object storage.

D. By optimizing content delivery through a Content Delivery Network (CDN).

Correct Answer: B

Feedback:

A Google Cloud "Folder" contributes to effective resource management by serving as an organizational unit for grouping projects and resources. It allows for a logical and flexible structure within an organization.

Q No. 7: Why is understanding the organization hierarchy important in Google Cloud Resource Management?

A. It enables the creation of virtual machines with customizable configurations.

B. It allows for efficient billing and monitoring of resource usage.

C. It facilitates real-time and batch processing of data.

D. It provides a centralized view for organizing and managing cloud resources.

Correct Answer: D

Feedback:

Understanding the organization hierarchy in Google Cloud Resource Management is important as it provides a centralized view for organizing and managing cloud resources within an organization.

Q No. 8: What is the significance of Google Cloud's Cloud Identity-Aware Proxy (IAP)?

A. To optimize content delivery through a Content Delivery Network (CDN).

B. To provide an additional layer of security for applications.

C. To create and run serverless functions that respond to events.

D. To manage and control access to Google Cloud resources.

Correct Answer: B

Feedback:

Google Cloud's Cloud Identity-Aware Proxy (IAP) is significant for providing an additional layer of security for applications. It verifies user identity and checks for authorization before granting access.

Q No. 9: How do Google Cloud Organization Policies contribute to compliance within an organization?

A. By optimizing content delivery through a Content Delivery Network (CDN).

B. By managing and resolving domain names for applications and services.

C. By enforcing rules and controls to ensure adherence to compliance standards.

D. By creating and running serverless functions that respond to events.

Correct Answer: C

Feedback:

Google Cloud Organization Policies contribute to compliance within an organization by enforcing rules and controls to ensure adherence to compliance standards.

Q No. 10: In the context of Google Cloud Resource Manager, what is the primary function of a "Project"?

A. To optimize content delivery through a Content Delivery Network (CDN).

B. To enable application modernization and management across hybrid and multi-cloud environments.

C. To encapsulate resources and services, defining the scope of billing and permissions.

D. To provide scalable and durable object storage.

Correct Answer: C

Feedback:

In the context of Google Cloud Resource Manager, the primary function of a "Project" is to encapsulate resources and services, defining the scope of billing and permissions within the organization hierarchy.

Q No. 11: What is the primary role of Cloud Resource Manager in Google Cloud?

A. To create and run serverless functions that respond to events.

B. To provide scalable and durable object storage.

C. To organize and manage cloud resources in a hierarchical structure.

D. To optimize content delivery through a Content Delivery Network (CDN).

Correct Answer: C

Feedback:

Cloud Resource Manager's primary role in Google Cloud is to organize and manage cloud resources in a hierarchical structure. It serves as a central hub for creating, tracking, and managing resources within an organization.

Q No. 12: How does Cloud Resource Manager contribute to visibility in Google Cloud?

A. By optimizing content delivery through a Content Delivery Network (CDN).

B. By providing identity services, user management, and access control.

C. By creating and running serverless functions that respond to events.

D. By offering a unified view of an organization's cloud assets.

Correct Answer: D

Feedback:

Cloud Resource Manager contributes to visibility in Google Cloud by offering a unified view of an organization's cloud assets. It provides a single pane of glass to oversee projects, manage permissions, and track usage.

Q No. 13: What is the purpose of a "Folder" in Google Cloud's organization hierarchy?

A. To enable application modernization and management across hybrid and multi-cloud environments.

B. To serve as an organizational unit for grouping projects and resources.

C. To provide scalable and durable object storage.

D. To create and run serverless functions that respond to events.

Correct Answer: B

Feedback:

A "Folder" in Google Cloud's organization hierarchy serves as an organizational unit for grouping projects and resources. It provides a flexible way to structure resources based on departments, teams, or projects.

Q No. 14 How does Cloud Resource Manager contribute to effective billing in Google Cloud?

A. By optimizing content delivery through a Content Delivery Network (CDN).

B. By providing identity services, user management, and access control.

C. By serving as a central hub for creating, tracking, and managing resources.

D. By defining the scope of billing and permissions within projects.

Correct Answer: C

Feedback:

Cloud Resource Manager contributes to effective billing in Google Cloud by serving as a central hub for creating, tracking, and managing resources. It provides visibility and organization for efficient billing.

Q No. 15: What is the primary purpose of Google Cloud's "Project" in the organization hierarchy?

A. To create and run serverless functions that respond to events.

B. To provide scalable and durable object storage.

C. To encapsulate resources and services, defining the scope of billing and permissions.

D. To optimize content delivery through a Content Delivery Network (CDN).

Correct Answer: C

Feedback:

The primary purpose of a Google Cloud "Project" in the organization hierarchy is to encapsulate resources and services, defining the scope of billing and permissions.

Q No. 16: How do Google Cloud "Projects" contribute to access control?

A. By providing identity services, user management, and access control.

B. By optimizing content delivery through a Content Delivery Network (CDN).

C. By creating and running serverless functions that respond to events.

D. By defining the scope of billing and permissions within an organization.

Correct Answer: A

Feedback:

Google Cloud "Projects" contribute to access control by providing identity services, user management, and access control. They establish a scope for permissions and access within the organization.

Q No. 17: Why is understanding the organization hierarchy crucial for effective resource management?

A. It allows for efficient billing and monitoring of resource usage.

B. It provides scalable and durable object storage.

C. It enables the creation of virtual machines with customizable configurations.

D. It facilitates real-time and batch processing of data.

Correct Answer: A

Feedback:

Understanding the organization hierarchy in Google Cloud is crucial for effective resource management as it allows for efficient billing and monitoring of resource usage within a structured framework.

Q No. 18: What is the role of Cloud Identity-Aware Proxy (IAP) in Google Cloud?

A. To manage and control access to Google Cloud resources.

B. To optimize content delivery through a Content Delivery Network (CDN).

C. To create and run serverless functions that respond to events.

D. To provide an additional layer of security for applications.

Correct Answer: D

Feedback:

The role of Cloud Identity-Aware Proxy (IAP) in Google Cloud is to provide an additional layer of security for applications. It verifies user identity and checks for authorization before granting access.

Q No. 19: How do Google Cloud Organization Policies contribute to governance?

A. By optimizing content delivery through a Content Delivery Network (CDN).

B. By enforcing rules and controls to ensure adherence to compliance standards.

C. By creating and running serverless functions that respond to events.

D. By managing and resolving domain names for applications and services.

Correct Answer: B

Feedback:

Google Cloud Organization Policies contribute to governance by enforcing rules and controls to ensure adherence to compliance standards within an organization.

Q No. 20: What is the primary function of Google Cloud's Cloud DNS?

A. To enable application modernization and management across hybrid and multi-cloud environments.

B. To create and run serverless functions that respond to events.

C. To manage and resolve domain names for applications and services.

D. To provide scalable and durable object storage.

Correct Answer: C

Feedback:

The primary function of Google Cloud's Cloud DNS is to manage and resolve domain names for applications and services. It provides a reliable and scalable domain name resolution service.

Q No. 21: How does a Google Cloud "Folder" enhance resource management efficiency?

A. By providing identity services, user management, and access control.

B. By serving as a centralized repository for object storage.

C. By facilitating communication and management of APIs.

D. By acting as an organizational unit for grouping projects and resources.

Correct Answer: D

Feedback:

A Google Cloud "Folder" enhances resource management efficiency by acting as an organizational unit for grouping projects and resources. It provides a logical structure for efficient resource organization.

Q No. 22: What is the significance of horizontal scaling in Google Cloud?

A. It involves adding more resources to a single virtual machine.

B. It enables the addition of more instances to distribute the load across multiple resources.

C. It refers to increasing the capacity of a single server.

D. It involves upgrading the hardware of a physical server.

Correct Answer: B

Feedback:

In Google Cloud, horizontal scaling involves adding more instances to distribute the load across multiple resources. It allows applications to handle increased workloads by adding more virtual machines or containers.

Q No. 23: In the context of Google Cloud, what is the primary purpose of Cloud CDN?

A. To provide scalable and durable object storage.

B. To optimize content delivery through a Content Delivery Network (CDN).

C. To create and run serverless functions that respond to events.

D. To manage and resolve domain names for applications and services.

Correct Answer: B

Feedback:

In the context of Google Cloud, the primary purpose of Cloud CDN is to optimize content delivery through a Content Delivery Network (CDN). It caches content at strategically located points of presence (PoPs) around the world.

Q No. 24: How does Cloud Armor contribute to security in Google Cloud?

A. By providing a fully managed file storage service.

B. By creating and running serverless functions that respond to events.

C. By optimizing content delivery through a Content Delivery Network (CDN).

D. By protecting applications and services from Distributed Denial of Service (DDoS) attacks.

Correct Answer: D

Feedback:

Cloud Armor in Google Cloud contributes to security by protecting applications and services from Distributed Denial of Service (DDoS) attacks. It provides security policies and defenses against malicious traffic.

Q No. 25: What is the role of Google Cloud's Anthos?

A. To provide scalable and durable object storage.

B. To enable application modernization and management across hybrid and multi-cloud environments.

C. To manage and control access to Google Cloud resources.

D. To create and run serverless functions that respond to events.

Correct Answer: B

Feedback:

The role of Google Cloud's Anthos is to enable application modernization and management across hybrid and multi-cloud environments. It allows organizations to build and deploy applications consistently across different environments.

Q No. 26: When creating a managed instance group, why is it important to use a health check?

A. To provide a private, isolated network within the public cloud.

B. To monitor and analyze the performance of applications and infrastructure.

C. To enable application modernization and management across hybrid and multi-cloud environments.

D. To ensure that only healthy instances receive traffic.

Correct Answer: D

Feedback:

When creating a managed instance group in Google Cloud, using a health check is important to ensure that only healthy instances receive traffic. Health checks monitor the status of instances and direct traffic away from instances that are not responding correctly.

Q No. 27: What is the primary purpose of Google Cloud's Cloud Dataflow?

A. To create virtual machines with customizable configurations.

B. To perform real-time and batch processing of data.

C. To optimize content delivery through a Content Delivery Network (CDN).

D. To enable application modernization and management across hybrid and multi-cloud environments.

Correct Answer: B

Feedback:

The primary purpose of Google Cloud's Cloud Dataflow is to perform real-time and batch processing of data. It allows the design and deployment of data processing pipelines for tasks like ETL (Extract, Transform, Load) and stream processing.

Q No. 28: How does Cloud Identity contribute to access management in Google Cloud?

A. By managing and resolving domain names for applications and services.

B. By optimizing content delivery through a Content Delivery Network (CDN).

C. By providing identity services, user management, and access control.

D. By creating and running serverless functions that respond to events.

Correct Answer: C

Feedback:

Cloud Identity in Google Cloud contributes to access management by providing identity services, user management, and access control. It establishes a centralized directory for managing users, groups, and devices.

Q No. 29: What is the role of Google Cloud's Cloud Endpoints?

A. To provide scalable and durable object storage.

B. To create and run serverless functions that respond to events.

C. To enable application modernization and management across hybrid and multi-cloud environments.

D. To facilitate communication and management of APIs.

Correct Answer: D

Feedback:

The role of Google Cloud's Cloud Endpoints is to facilitate communication and management of APIs. It allows for the creation, deployment, and management of scalable and secure APIs.

Q No. 30: In the context of Google Cloud, what is the purpose of Cloud Storage Nearline?

A. To enable application modernization and management across hybrid and multi-cloud environments.

B. To perform real-time and batch processing of data.

C. To provide scalable and durable object storage for infrequently accessed data.

D. To manage and resolve domain names for applications and services.

Correct Answer: C

Feedback:

In the context of Google Cloud, the purpose of Cloud Storage Nearline is to provide scalable and durable object storage for infrequently accessed data. It offers a cost-effective solution for long-term storage.

Chapter 5: Cloud Identity and Access Management

In the ever-evolving landscape of cloud computing, ensuring robust security and access controls is paramount. Google Cloud's Identity and Access Management (IAM) plays a pivotal role in safeguarding resources and data. This chapter provides an in-depth exploration of Cloud IAM, covering its overview, components, and the critical aspects of members, roles, policies, conditions, and compliance.

Cloud IAM Overview

Introduction:

Cloud IAM is the foundation of access control within Google Cloud. It empowers organizations to manage permissions and control access to resources securely. This section offers a comprehensive overview of Cloud IAM, emphasizing its significance in ensuring a secure and well-managed cloud environment.

Key Concepts:

Understanding the fundamental concepts of Cloud IAM, including members, roles, and policies, is essential for implementing effective access controls. This chapter delves into these key concepts, providing clarity on how they interconnect to form a robust security framework.

Members, Roles, and Policies

Google Accounts:

Google Accounts are the starting point for identity management in Cloud IAM. This section elucidates the role of Google Accounts in establishing user identities and the linkage to resource access within Google Cloud.

Groups:

Groups simplify the process of managing and assigning permissions to multiple users. This section explores the creation and utilization of groups for streamlined access control.

Service Accounts:

Service accounts are pivotal for non-human entities, such as applications and virtual machines, to interact with Google Cloud services. Understanding their role and implementation is crucial for comprehensive IAM management.

IAM Roles:

IAM roles define a set of permissions that determine what actions can be performed on specified resources. This section provides an in-depth examination of IAM roles, their types, and their implications for access control.

IAM Policies:

IAM policies encapsulate the permissions granted to members through roles. This section explores the creation, modification, and enforcement of IAM policies to achieve fine-grained control over resource access.

IAM Conditions

Introduction to IAM Conditions:

IAM Conditions introduce an additional layer of control by allowing policies to be applied based on specific conditions. This section explores the implementation of IAM Conditions and their role in enhancing security.

Use Cases:

Real-world use cases highlight the practical application of IAM Conditions. From time-based access controls to location-based policies, these examples showcase the versatility and flexibility of IAM Conditions.

Accounting and Technical Compliance

Monitoring and Auditing:

Effective IAM goes beyond access control; it involves monitoring and auditing to ensure compliance. This section delves into the tools and practices for monitoring IAM activities and auditing permissions to maintain a secure environment.

Compliance Frameworks:

Google Cloud adheres to various compliance frameworks, and understanding how IAM aligns with these frameworks is crucial for organizations with specific regulatory requirements. This section explores the compliance landscape and IAM's role in meeting these standards.

Best Practices:

Implementing IAM best practices is fundamental for maintaining a secure and compliant environment. This section provides practical guidance on configuration, monitoring, and ongoing management to optimize IAM implementation.

Cloud IAM stands as the linchpin for security and access management in Google Cloud. This chapter has provided a comprehensive exploration of IAM, covering its foundational concepts, key components, advanced features like IAM Conditions, and the critical aspects of compliance. As organizations navigate the complex terrain of cloud security, mastering IAM is imperative for achieving a balance between accessibility and control.

Practice Exam Questions and Answers

Q No. 1: What is the primary purpose of Google Cloud's Identity and Access Management (IAM)?

A. To create and manage virtual machines.

B. To organize and manage cloud resources in a hierarchical structure.

C. To optimize content delivery through a Content Delivery Network (CDN).

D. To manage permissions and control access to resources securely.

Correct Answer: D

Feedback:

Google Cloud's IAM is designed to manage permissions and control access to resources securely within the cloud environment.

Q No. 2: What is the role of IAM roles in Google Cloud?

A. To create and run serverless functions that respond to events.

B. To encapsulate resources and services, defining the scope of billing and permissions.

C. To provide scalable and durable object storage.

D. To define a set of permissions that determine what actions can be performed on specified resources.

Correct Answer: D

Feedback:

IAM roles in Google Cloud define a set of permissions that determine what actions can be performed on specified resources.

Q No. 3: How do Google Accounts contribute to Cloud IAM?

A. By providing identity services, user management, and access control.

B. By serving as a central hub for creating, tracking, and managing resources.

C. By organizing resources in a hierarchical structure.

D. By establishing user identities and linking them to resource access.

Correct Answer: D

Feedback:

Google Accounts contribute to Cloud IAM by establishing user identities and linking them to resource access within Google Cloud.

Q No. 4: What is the significance of IAM policies?

A. To provide scalable and durable object storage.

B. To organize and manage cloud resources in a hierarchical structure.

C. To create and run serverless functions that respond to events.

D. To encapsulate the permissions granted to members through roles.

Correct Answer: D

Feedback:

IAM policies in Google Cloud encapsulate the permissions granted to members through roles, defining the access control for resources.

Q No. 5: How do IAM Conditions enhance access control in Google Cloud?

A. By creating and running serverless functions that respond to events.

B. By optimizing content delivery through a Content Delivery Network (CDN).

C. By allowing policies to be applied based on specific conditions.

D. By managing and resolving domain names for applications and services.

Correct Answer: C

Feedback:

IAM Conditions in Google Cloud enhance access control by allowing policies to be applied based on specific conditions, providing an additional layer of control.

Q No. 6: Why are groups useful in Cloud IAM?

A. To optimize content delivery through a Content Delivery Network (CDN).

B. To serve as a centralized repository for object storage.

C. To facilitate communication and management of APIs.

D. To simplify the process of managing and assigning permissions to multiple users.

Correct Answer: D

Feedback:

Groups in Cloud IAM are useful to simplify the process of managing and assigning permissions to multiple users, promoting streamlined access control.

Q No. 7: What is the primary function of Google Cloud's Cloud Armor?

A. To optimize content delivery through a Content Delivery Network (CDN).

B. To provide fully managed file storage services.

C. To protect applications and services from Distributed Denial of Service (DDoS) attacks.

D. To enable application modernization and management across hybrid and multi-cloud environments.

Correct Answer: C

Feedback:

The primary function of Google Cloud's Cloud Armor is to protect applications and services from Distributed Denial of Service (DDoS) attacks.

Q No. 8: How does Cloud IAM contribute to technical compliance in Google Cloud?

A. By creating and running serverless functions that respond to events.

B. By enforcing rules and controls to ensure adherence to compliance standards.

C. By optimizing content delivery through a Content Delivery Network (CDN).

D. By providing identity services, user management, and access control.

Correct Answer: B

Feedback:

Cloud IAM contributes to technical compliance in Google Cloud by enforcing rules and controls to ensure adherence to compliance standards within an organization.

Q No. 9: What role do Service Accounts play in Cloud IAM?

A. To provide scalable and durable object storage.

B. To create and manage virtual machines.

C. To facilitate communication and management of APIs.

D. To allow non-human entities, such as applications, to interact with Google Cloud services.

Correct Answer: D

Feedback:

Service Accounts in Cloud IAM play a role in allowing non-human entities, such as applications, to interact with Google Cloud services securely.

Q No. 10: How does IAM auditing contribute to compliance in Google Cloud?

A. By providing identity services, user management, and access control.

B. By optimizing content delivery through a Content Delivery Network (CDN).

C. By monitoring and auditing IAM activities to ensure compliance.

D. By creating and running serverless functions that respond to events.

Correct Answer: C

Feedback:

IAM auditing in Google Cloud contributes to compliance by monitoring and auditing IAM activities, ensuring adherence to security and compliance standards.

Q No. 11: What is the purpose of IAM Conditions in Google Cloud's Identity and Access Management?

A. To create and manage virtual machines.

B. To allow policies to be applied based on specific conditions.

C. To optimize content delivery through a Content Delivery Network (CDN).

D. To manage permissions for service accounts.

Correct Answer: B

Feedback:

IAM Conditions in Google Cloud's IAM allow policies to be applied based on specific conditions, adding an extra layer of control to access management.

Q No. 12: How does Cloud IAM contribute to access control for non-human entities in Google Cloud?

A. By creating and running serverless functions that respond to events.

B. By providing scalable and durable object storage.

C. By managing permissions for service accounts.

D. By optimizing content delivery through a Content Delivery Network (CDN).

Correct Answer: C

Feedback:

Cloud IAM in Google Cloud contributes to access control for non-human entities, such as applications, by managing permissions for service accounts.

Q No. 13: What role do Google Cloud's IAM roles play in achieving fine-grained access control?

A. To optimize content delivery through a Content Delivery Network (CDN).

B. To define a set of permissions that determine what actions can be performed on specified resources.

C. To organize and manage cloud resources in a hierarchical structure.

D. To create and manage virtual machines.

Correct Answer: B

Feedback:

Google Cloud's IAM roles play a role in achieving fine-grained access control by defining a set of permissions for specific actions on specified resources.

Q No. 14: In the context of Google Cloud IAM, what is the primary function of IAM policies?

A. To provide scalable and durable object storage.

B. To organize and manage cloud resources in a hierarchical structure.

C. To create and run serverless functions that respond to events.

D. To encapsulate the permissions granted to members through roles.

Correct Answer: D

Feedback:

In the context of Google Cloud IAM, IAM policies encapsulate the permissions granted to members through roles, defining the access control for resources.

Q No. 15: How does Cloud IAM contribute to security in Google Cloud?

A. By optimizing content delivery through a Content Delivery Network (CDN).

B. By managing and resolving domain names for applications and services.

C. By defining, managing, and auditing access to resources securely.

D. By creating and running serverless functions that respond to events.

Correct Answer: C

Feedback:

Cloud IAM contributes to security in Google Cloud by defining, managing, and auditing access to resources securely, ensuring proper access controls.

Q No. 16: What is the primary purpose of Cloud Identity and Access Management in Google Cloud?

A. To optimize content delivery through a Content Delivery Network (CDN).

B. To manage permissions and control access to resources securely.

C. To create and manage virtual machines.

D. To provide scalable and durable object storage.

Correct Answer: B

Feedback:

The primary purpose of Cloud Identity and Access Management (IAM) in Google Cloud is to manage permissions and control access to resources securely.

Q No. 17: Why are IAM Conditions useful in Google Cloud's IAM?

A. To manage and resolve domain names for applications and services.

B. To allow policies to be applied based on specific conditions.

C. To provide scalable and durable object storage.

D. To optimize content delivery through a Content Delivery Network (CDN).

Correct Answer: B

Feedback:

IAM Conditions in Google Cloud's IAM are useful to allow policies to be applied based on specific conditions, offering granular control over access.

Q No. 18: How does IAM auditing contribute to compliance in Google Cloud?

A. By optimizing content delivery through a Content Delivery Network (CDN).

B. By providing identity services, user management, and access control.

C. By monitoring and auditing IAM activities to ensure compliance.

D. By creating and running serverless functions that respond to events.

Correct Answer: C

Feedback:

IAM auditing in Google Cloud contributes to compliance by monitoring and auditing IAM activities, ensuring adherence to security and compliance standards.

Q No. 19: What is the role of Google Groups in Cloud IAM?

A. To optimize content delivery through a Content Delivery Network (CDN).

B. To serve as a centralized repository for object storage.

C. To simplify the process of managing and assigning permissions to multiple users.

D. To create and run serverless functions that respond to events.

Correct Answer: C

Feedback:

Google Groups in Cloud IAM play a role in simplifying the process of managing and assigning permissions to multiple users, promoting streamlined access control.

Q No. 20: How does Cloud IAM contribute to efficient access management for multiple users?

A. By providing identity services, user management, and access control.

B. By optimizing content delivery through a Content Delivery Network (CDN).

C. By creating and running serverless functions that respond to events.

D. By using Google Groups to manage permissions centrally.

Correct Answer: D

Feedback:

Cloud IAM in Google Cloud contributes to efficient access management for multiple users by using Google Groups to manage permissions centrally.

Q No. 21: What is the significance of IAM roles in the context of resource access in Google Cloud?

A. To create and run serverless functions that respond to events.

B. To encapsulate the permissions granted to members through roles.

C. To manage permissions and control access to resources securely.

D. To optimize content delivery through a Content Delivery Network (CDN).

Correct Answer: B

Feedback:

IAM roles in Google Cloud are significant for encapsulating the permissions granted to members through roles, defining access controls for resources.

Q No. 22: How does IAM Conditions contribute to dynamic access control in Google Cloud?

A. By creating and running serverless functions that respond to events.

B. By allowing policies to be applied based on specific conditions, providing dynamic access control.

C. By optimizing content delivery through a Content Delivery Network (CDN).

D. By managing and resolving domain names for applications and services.

Correct Answer: B

Feedback:

IAM Conditions in Google Cloud contribute to dynamic access control by allowing policies to be applied based on specific conditions, adapting to varying scenarios.

Q No. 23: Why is IAM auditing crucial for security in Google Cloud?

A. By providing identity services, user management, and access control.

B. By optimizing content delivery through a Content Delivery Network (CDN).

C. By monitoring and auditing IAM activities to identify and respond to security incidents.

D. By creating and running serverless functions that respond to events.

Correct Answer: C

Feedback:

IAM auditing in Google Cloud is crucial for security by monitoring and auditing IAM activities, enabling the identification and response to security incidents.

Q No. 24: What is the primary role of Service Accounts in Google Cloud IAM?

A. To optimize content delivery through a Content Delivery Network (CDN).

B. To create and manage virtual machines.

C. To allow non-human entities, such as applications, to interact with Google Cloud services securely.

D. To manage permissions for user accounts.

Correct Answer: C

Feedback:

The primary role of Service Accounts in Google Cloud IAM is to allow non-human entities, such as applications, to interact with Google Cloud services securely.

Q No. 25: How does IAM Conditions contribute to access control flexibility in Google Cloud?

A. By optimizing content delivery through a Content Delivery Network (CDN).

B. By allowing policies to be applied based on specific conditions, providing flexibility in access control.

C. By creating and running serverless functions that respond to events.

D. By managing and resolving domain names for applications and services.

Correct Answer: B

Feedback:

IAM Conditions in Google Cloud contribute to access control flexibility by allowing policies to be applied based on specific conditions, adapting to diverse scenarios.

Q No. 26: In the context of Google Cloud IAM, why are IAM roles considered essential?

A. To create and run serverless functions that respond to events.

B. To define a set of permissions that determine what actions can be performed on specified resources.

C. To manage permissions for user accounts.

D. To optimize content delivery through a Content Delivery Network (CDN).

Correct Answer: B

Feedback:

IAM roles in Google Cloud IAM are considered essential for defining a set of permissions that determine what actions can be performed on specified resources.

Q No. 27: What is the primary purpose of Cloud IAM in Google Cloud?

A. To create and manage virtual machines.

B. To manage permissions and control access to resources securely.

C. To optimize content delivery through a Content Delivery Network (CDN).

D. To organize and manage cloud resources in a hierarchical structure.

Correct Answer: B

Feedback:

The primary purpose of Cloud IAM in Google Cloud is to manage permissions and control access to resources securely within the cloud environment.

Q No. 28: How do IAM Conditions contribute to security in Google Cloud IAM?

A. By optimizing content delivery through a Content Delivery Network (CDN).

B. By allowing policies to be applied based on specific conditions, adding an additional layer of security.

C. By monitoring and auditing IAM activities for security incidents.

D. By creating and running serverless functions that respond to events.

Correct Answer: B

Feedback:

IAM Conditions in Google Cloud IAM contribute to security by allowing policies to be applied based on specific conditions, adding an additional layer of security to access controls.

Chapter 6: Networking

In the ever-expanding landscape of cloud computing, networking forms the backbone of infrastructure, determining how data flows, applications communicate, and services interact. Google Cloud's robust networking capabilities are designed to provide a seamless and secure environment for your applications. This chapter delves into the intricacies of Google Cloud's networking services, covering a range of topics from the foundational elements to advanced security measures.

Networking Deep Dive

Google's Global Network:

Explore the architecture and advantages of Google's global network. This section provides insights into how Google's vast network infrastructure contributes to low-latency and high-performance communication across the globe.

Network Tiers:

Understand the different network tiers available in Google Cloud and how they cater to diverse performance and cost requirements. This section provides a comparative analysis to help users choose the most suitable network tier for their applications.

Virtual Private Cloud (VPC), Subnets, Regions, and Zones

Virtual Private Cloud:

Dive into the concept of Virtual Private Clouds, the fundamental building blocks for organizing and isolating network resources. Learn how VPCs provide a secure and isolated space for your Google Cloud projects.

Subnet Ranges and IP Addressing:

Gain insights into subnetting strategies, IP address allocation, and the importance of designing efficient IP addressing schemes within VPCs.

Routes and Firewall Rules

Routes and Firewall Rules:

Understand the role of routes and firewall rules in controlling traffic within a VPC. Explore how these components contribute to secure and efficient communication between instances.

Private Access:

Learn about enabling private access to Google Cloud services, allowing instances within a VPC to access Google APIs and services without public IP addresses.

Cross-Project Communication:

Explore techniques for facilitating communication between resources across different Google Cloud projects, enabling collaboration and resource sharing.

Cloud DNS:

Discover the capabilities of Cloud DNS for managing domain names and providing scalable and reliable domain resolution services within Google Cloud.

Connectivity to Your Cloud

Cloud Router:

Examine the role of Cloud Router in dynamically exchanging routes between your on-premises network and Google Cloud, enabling seamless connectivity.

Cloud VPN:

Learn how Cloud VPN provides a secure connection between your on-premises network and your VPC, extending your network to the cloud securely.

Cloud Interconnect:

Explore the benefits of Cloud Interconnect, which provides dedicated and reliable connections between your on-premises network and Google Cloud, suitable for high-bandwidth and low-latency requirements.

Cloud Load Balancing

Cloud Load Balancing:

Understand how Cloud Load Balancing distributes incoming traffic across multiple instances to ensure optimal resource utilization and application performance.

Network Security

Network Security Principles:

Explore foundational principles for securing your Google Cloud network, including the principle of least privilege and defense in depth.

Google Front End:

Learn about the Google Front End (GFE) and its role in handling SSL/TLS termination and load balancing, enhancing the security and performance of your applications.

Firewalls:

Understand how Google Cloud's firewalls provide a powerful mechanism for controlling traffic to and from your instances, safeguarding your applications and data.

Cloud Armor:

Dive into Cloud Armor, Google Cloud's DDoS and application defense service, protecting your applications from external threats and attacks.

Cloud NAT:

Explore Cloud NAT, a service that allows instances in a private subnet to access the internet while keeping the source IP addresses hidden.

VPC Service Controls:

Understand how VPC Service Controls enhance security by providing additional controls over data access within Google Cloud services.

Identity-Aware Proxy:

Explore Identity-Aware Proxy (IAP), a service that provides context-aware access controls to applications running on Google Cloud.

Network Logging:

Learn about the importance of network logging for monitoring and auditing network activities, facilitating incident response and compliance.

From the foundational elements of VPCs, subnets, and IP addressing to advanced security measures like Cloud Armor and Identity-Aware Proxy, this chapter equips you with the knowledge to architect a secure, performant, and scalable network infrastructure on Google Cloud.

Practice Exam Questions and Answers

Q No. 1: What is the primary purpose of Google's global network in the context of Google Cloud?

A. To provide scalable and durable object storage.

B. To optimize content delivery through a Content Delivery Network (CDN).

C. To manage permissions and control access to resources securely.

D. To ensure low-latency and high-performance communication across the globe.

Correct Answer: D

Explanation:

Google's global network is designed to ensure low-latency and high-performance communication across the globe, providing a robust infrastructure for Google Cloud services.

Q No. 2: What is the significance of Virtual Private Clouds (VPCs) in Google Cloud?

A. To create and manage virtual machines.

B. To manage permissions and control access to resources securely.

C. To organize and isolate network resources within Google Cloud.

D. To optimize content delivery through a Content Delivery Network (CDN).

Correct Answer: C

Explanation:

VPCs in Google Cloud play a significant role in organizing and isolating network resources, providing a secure and isolated space for projects.

Q No. 3: How does Cloud Router contribute to connectivity between on-premises networks and Google Cloud?

A. By creating and running serverless functions that respond to events.

B. By facilitating dynamic exchange of routes between on-premises networks and Google Cloud VPCs.

C. By optimizing content delivery through a Content Delivery Network (CDN).

D. By managing permissions for service accounts.

Correct Answer: B

Explanation:

Cloud Router facilitates the dynamic exchange of routes between on-premises networks and Google Cloud VPCs, ensuring seamless connectivity.

Q No. 4: What is the purpose of Cloud Load Balancing in Google Cloud?

A. To optimize content delivery through a Content Delivery Network (CDN).

B. To provide scalable and durable object storage.

C. To distribute incoming traffic across multiple instances for optimal resource utilization.

D. To create and run serverless functions that respond to events.

Correct Answer: C

Explanation:

Cloud Load Balancing in Google Cloud is designed to distribute incoming traffic across multiple instances, ensuring optimal resource utilization and application performance.

Q No. 5: How does Cloud Armor contribute to security in Google Cloud?

A. By optimizing content delivery through a Content Delivery Network (CDN).

B. By providing fully managed file storage services.

C. By protecting applications and services from Distributed Denial of Service (DDoS) attacks.

D. By creating and running serverless functions that respond to events.

Correct Answer: C

Explanation:

Cloud Armor in Google Cloud contributes to security by protecting applications and services from Distributed Denial of Service (DDoS) attacks.

Q No. 6: What role do firewall rules play in Google Cloud's networking security?

A. To create and manage virtual machines.

B. To encapsulate the permissions granted to members through roles.

C. To define policies for controlling traffic to and from instances.

D. To optimize content delivery through a Content Delivery Network (CDN).

Correct Answer: C

Explanation:

Firewall rules in Google Cloud's networking security play a role in defining policies for controlling traffic to and from instances, ensuring secure communication.

Q No. 7: How does Cloud Interconnect differ from Cloud VPN in Google Cloud?

A. Cloud Interconnect provides secure connections between on-premises networks and Google Cloud, suitable for high-bandwidth and low-latency requirements.

B. Cloud VPN facilitates a secure connection between on-premises networks and Google Cloud VPCs.

C. Cloud Interconnect is designed for low-latency communication within a VPC.

D. Cloud VPN is optimized for high-bandwidth communication within a VPC.

Correct Answer: A

Explanation:

Cloud Interconnect provides dedicated and reliable connections between on-premises networks and Google Cloud, suitable for high-bandwidth and low-latency requirements.

Q No. 8: What is the primary function of Cloud NAT in Google Cloud?

A. To optimize content delivery through a Content Delivery Network (CDN).

B. To allow non-human entities, such as applications, to interact with Google Cloud services securely.

C. To provide scalable and durable object storage.

D. To enable instances in a private subnet to access the internet while keeping source IP addresses hidden.

Correct Answer: D

Explanation:

The primary function of Cloud NAT in Google Cloud is to enable instances in a private subnet to access the internet while keeping source IP addresses hidden.

Q No. 9: How does VPC Service Controls enhance security in Google Cloud?

A. By optimizing content delivery through a Content Delivery Network (CDN).

B. By providing identity services, user management, and access control.

C. By enforcing additional controls over data access within Google Cloud services.

D. By creating and running serverless functions that respond to events.

Correct Answer: C

Explanation:

VPC Service Controls in Google Cloud enhance security by providing additional controls over data access within Google Cloud services.

Q No. 10: What is the role of Identity-Aware Proxy (IAP) in Google Cloud's networking security?

A. To optimize content delivery through a Content Delivery Network (CDN).

B. To facilitate communication and management of APIs.

C. To create and manage virtual machines.

D. To provide context-aware access controls to applications running on Google Cloud.

Correct Answer: D

Explanation:

Identity-Aware Proxy (IAP) in Google Cloud's networking security provides context-aware access controls to applications running on Google Cloud.

Q No. 11: How does Google's Global Network contribute to the performance of Google Cloud services?

A. By optimizing content delivery through a Content Delivery Network (CDN).

B. By providing low-latency and high-performance communication across the globe.

C. By managing permissions and control access to resources securely.

D. By creating and running serverless functions that respond to events.

Correct Answer: B

Explanation:

Google's Global Network ensures low-latency and high-performance communication across the globe, enhancing the performance of Google Cloud services.

Q No. 12: What is the purpose of Network Tiers in Google Cloud?

A. To optimize content delivery through a Content Delivery Network (CDN).

B. To define a set of permissions that determine what actions can be performed on specified resources.

C. To manage permissions and control access to resources securely.

D. To offer different levels of network performance and cost options.

Correct Answer: D

Explanation:

Network Tiers in Google Cloud provide different levels of network performance and cost options, allowing users to choose the most suitable tier for their requirements.

Q No. 13: In the context of Virtual Private Clouds (VPCs), what is the purpose of Subnets?

A. To create and manage virtual machines.

B. To organize and isolate network resources within a VPC.

C. To provide scalable and durable object storage.

D. To optimize content delivery through a Content Delivery Network (CDN).

Correct Answer: B

Explanation:

Subnets in VPCs are used to organize and isolate network resources within a VPC, providing a secure and segmented environment.

Q No. 14: How do Routes and Firewall Rules work together in Google Cloud's networking?

A. Routes define the path for traffic, and Firewall Rules control the traffic flow to and from instances.

B. Routes manage permissions, and Firewall Rules optimize content delivery.

C. Routes and Firewall Rules are synonymous terms.

D. Routes and Firewall Rules are independent of each other in Google Cloud.

Correct Answer: A

Explanation:

Routes define the path for traffic, and Firewall Rules control the traffic flow to and from instances in Google Cloud's networking.

Q No. 15: What is the significance of Private Access in Google Cloud's networking?

A. To optimize content delivery through a Content Delivery Network (CDN).

B. To allow instances within a VPC to access Google APIs and services without public IP addresses.

C. To manage permissions and control access to resources securely.

D. To create and run serverless functions that respond to events.

Correct Answer: B

Explanation:

Private Access in Google Cloud's networking allows instances within a VPC to access Google APIs and services without public IP addresses, enhancing security.

Q No. 16: Why is Cloud Router essential for connectivity between on-premises networks and Google Cloud?

A. By creating and running serverless functions that respond to events.

B. By facilitating dynamic exchange of routes between on-premises networks and Google Cloud VPCs.

C. By optimizing content delivery through a Content Delivery Network (CDN).

D. By managing permissions for service accounts.

Correct Answer: B

Explanation:

Cloud Router is essential for facilitating the dynamic exchange of routes between on-premises networks and Google Cloud VPCs, ensuring seamless connectivity.

Q No. 17: How does Cloud Load Balancing contribute to the reliability of applications in Google Cloud?

A. By optimizing content delivery through a Content Delivery Network (CDN).

B. By providing scalable and durable object storage.

C. By distributing incoming traffic across multiple instances for optimal resource utilization.

D. By creating and running serverless functions that respond to events.

Correct Answer: C

Explanation:

Cloud Load Balancing in Google Cloud contributes to the reliability of applications by distributing incoming traffic across multiple instances for optimal resource utilization.

Q No. 18: What is the primary function of Cloud Armor in Google Cloud's networking security?

A. To optimize content delivery through a Content Delivery Network (CDN).

B. To protect applications and services from Distributed Denial of Service (DDoS) attacks.

C. To provide scalable and durable object storage.

D. To enable instances in a private subnet to access the internet securely.

Correct Answer: B

Explanation:

The primary function of Cloud Armor in Google Cloud's networking security is to protect applications and services from Distributed Denial of Service (DDoS) attacks.

Q No. 19: How does Cloud NAT enhance privacy and security in Google Cloud?

A. By optimizing content delivery through a Content Delivery Network (CDN).

B. By managing and resolving domain names for applications and services.

C. By enabling instances in a private subnet to access the internet while keeping source IP addresses hidden.

D. By creating and running serverless functions that respond to events.

Correct Answer: C

Explanation:

Cloud NAT enhances privacy and security in Google Cloud by enabling instances in a private subnet to access the internet while keeping source IP addresses hidden.

Q No. 20: What is the role of Identity-Aware Proxy (IAP) in Google Cloud's networking security?

A. To optimize content delivery through a Content Delivery Network (CDN).

B. To facilitate communication and management of APIs.

C. To create and manage virtual machines.

D. To provide context-aware access controls to applications running on Google Cloud.

Correct Answer: D

Explanation:

Identity-Aware Proxy (IAP) in Google Cloud's networking security provides context-aware access controls to applications running on Google Cloud.

Q No. 21: How does VPC Service Controls contribute to securing data access in Google Cloud services?

A. By optimizing content delivery through a Content Delivery Network (CDN).

B. By providing identity services, user management, and access control.

C. By enforcing additional controls over data access within Google Cloud services.

D. By creating and running serverless functions that respond to events.

Correct Answer: C

Explanation:

VPC Service Controls in Google Cloud contribute to securing data access by enforcing additional controls within Google Cloud services.

Q No. 22: What is the primary purpose of Google Front End in Google Cloud's networking?

A. To optimize content delivery through a Content Delivery Network (CDN).

B. To provide fully managed file storage services.

C. To protect applications and services from Distributed Denial of Service (DDoS) attacks.

D. To enable instances in a private subnet to access the internet securely.

Correct Answer: A

Explanation:

The primary purpose of Google Front End in Google Cloud's networking is to optimize content delivery through a Content Delivery Network (CDN).

Q No. 23: How does Cloud DNS contribute to domain name resolution in Google Cloud?

A. By optimizing content delivery through a Content Delivery Network (CDN).

B. By serving as a centralized repository for object storage.

C. By managing and resolving domain names for applications and services.

D. By creating and running serverless functions that respond to events.

Correct Answer: C

Explanation:

Cloud DNS in Google Cloud contributes to domain name resolution by managing and resolving domain names for applications and services.

Chapter 7: Compute and Containers

In this chapter, we will explore the diverse compute and containerization services offered by Google Cloud. These services provide a foundation for deploying and managing applications at scale, from virtual machines to serverless computing. Understanding the nuances of Google Compute Engine, App Engine, Kubernetes Engine, Cloud Functions, Cloud Run, and API Management is crucial for building resilient, scalable, and efficient applications on Google Cloud.

Google Compute Engine

Virtual Machine Instances:

Delve into the world of virtual machine instances on Google Compute Engine. Learn how to create, configure, and manage virtual machines to run your applications efficiently.

Images:

Understand the concept of images in Google Compute Engine, exploring how they serve as templates for virtual machine instances, enabling consistency and reproducibility.

Instance Templates and Instance Groups:

Explore the benefits of using instance templates and instance groups for managing and scaling virtual machine instances in a cost-effective and resilient manner.

Storage Options:

Discover the diverse storage options available on Google Compute Engine, from standard persistent disks to advanced solutions like Cloud Storage and Cloud Filestore.

OS Login:

Learn about OS Login, a secure way to manage access to virtual machine instances using Google Cloud Identity and Access Management (IAM).

Google App Engine

App Engine Flex vs. App Engine Standard:

Compare and contrast Google App Engine Flex and App Engine Standard, understanding the strengths and use cases of each platform for deploying and managing applications.

Google Kubernetes Engine

Cluster Architecture:

Dive into the architecture of Google Kubernetes Engine (GKE), understanding how clusters are structured and the roles played by master and worker nodes.

Configuration:

Explore the configuration options available for Google Kubernetes Engine, including cluster configuration, node pools, and workload deployment strategies.

Node Upgrades:

Understand the process of upgrading nodes in a Google Kubernetes Engine cluster, ensuring the reliability and security of your containerized applications.

Cloud Functions

Explore serverless computing with Google Cloud Functions. Learn how to create, deploy, and manage lightweight, event-driven functions that scale automatically.

Cloud Run

Discover Cloud Run, Google Cloud's fully managed compute platform for containerized applications. Explore the benefits of serverless containers and how Cloud Run simplifies deployment and scaling.

API Management

Apigee:

Learn about Apigee, Google Cloud's comprehensive API management platform. Understand how Apigee facilitates API design, deployment, security, and analytics.

Cloud Endpoints:

Explore Cloud Endpoints, a fully managed API gateway that enables you to create, deploy, and manage APIs securely.

Secure Your APIs:

Dive into best practices and tools for securing your APIs, covering aspects such as authentication, authorization, and encryption to ensure the integrity and confidentiality of your data.

From virtual machines on Compute Engine to serverless computing with Cloud Functions and container orchestration with Kubernetes Engine, you now have a comprehensive understanding of the tools at your disposal for deploying and managing applications on Google Cloud.

Practice Exam Questions and Answers

Q No. 1: What is the primary purpose of Google Compute Engine's instance templates?

A. To create virtual machine instances.

B. To serve as a template for creating virtual machine images.

C. To define a set of rules for firewall configurations.

D. To manage and scale virtual machine instances efficiently.

Correct Answer: D

Explanation:

Instance templates in Google Compute Engine are used to define a set of rules for creating and managing virtual machine instances efficiently, facilitating scalability.

Q No. 2: How does OS Login enhance security on Google Compute Engine?

A. By providing scalable and durable object storage.

B. By managing permissions for service accounts.

C. By allowing secure access to virtual machine instances using Google Cloud Identity and Access Management (IAM).

D. By optimizing content delivery through a Content Delivery Network (CDN).

Correct Answer: C

Explanation:

OS Login enhances security on Google Compute Engine by allowing secure access to virtual machine instances using Google Cloud Identity and Access Management (IAM).

Q No. 3: In the context of Google App Engine, what distinguishes App Engine Flex from App Engine Standard?

A. App Engine Flex allows automatic scaling based on demand, while App Engine Standard provides manual scaling.

B. App Engine Flex supports custom runtimes, while App Engine Standard supports only predefined runtimes.

C. App Engine Flex is suitable for containerized applications, while App Engine Standard is designed for stateless, serverless applications.

D. App Engine Flex is fully managed, while App Engine Standard requires manual management of infrastructure.

Correct Answer: C

Explanation:

App Engine Flex is suitable for containerized applications, providing flexibility and customization, while App Engine Standard is designed for stateless, serverless applications with automatic scaling.

Q No. 4: What is the primary function of Cloud Functions in Google Cloud?

A. To create and manage virtual machines.

B. To deploy and manage containerized applications.

C. To run lightweight, event-driven functions without the need for server management.

D. To provide fully managed file storage services.

Correct Answer: C

Explanation:

Cloud Functions in Google Cloud is designed to run lightweight, event-driven functions without the need for server management, providing a serverless computing environment.

Q No. 5: How does Cloud Run simplify the deployment of containerized applications on Google Cloud?

A. By providing scalable and durable object storage.

B. By automating the creation of virtual machine instances.

C. By offering fully managed, serverless containers that automatically scale.

D. By optimizing content delivery through a Content Delivery Network (CDN).

Correct Answer: C

Explanation:

Cloud Run simplifies the deployment of containerized applications on Google Cloud by offering fully managed, serverless containers that automatically scale based on demand.

Q No. 6: What is the role of Apigee in API management on Google Cloud?

A. To optimize content delivery through a Content Delivery Network (CDN).

B. To provide fully managed file storage services.

C. To facilitate API design, deployment, security, and analytics.

D. To manage permissions for service accounts.

Correct Answer: C

Explanation:

Apigee in Google Cloud serves as a comprehensive API management platform, facilitating API design, deployment, security, and analytics.

Q No. 7: How does Cloud Endpoints contribute to API management on Google Cloud?

A. By providing scalable and durable object storage.

B. By optimizing content delivery through a Content Delivery Network (CDN).

C. By creating and running serverless functions that respond to events.

D. By enabling you to create, deploy, and manage APIs securely.

Correct Answer: D

Explanation:

Cloud Endpoints in Google Cloud contributes to API management by enabling you to create, deploy, and manage APIs securely.

Q No. 8: What is the purpose of Cloud NAT in Google Cloud?

A. To create and manage virtual machines.

B. To allow non-human entities, such as applications, to interact with Google Cloud services securely.

C. To provide scalable and durable object storage.

D. To enable instances in a private subnet to access the internet while keeping source IP addresses hidden.

Correct Answer: D

Explanation:

The purpose of Cloud NAT in Google Cloud is to enable instances in a private subnet to access the internet while keeping source IP addresses hidden.

Q No. 9: In Google Kubernetes Engine (GKE), what is the role of master nodes?

A. To run containerized applications.

B. To manage and orchestrate containers in the cluster.

C. To facilitate communication between nodes.

D. To provide scalable and durable object storage.

Correct Answer: B

Explanation:

In Google Kubernetes Engine (GKE), master nodes manage and orchestrate containers in the cluster, handling tasks such as scheduling and scaling.

Q No. 10: What is the significance of instance groups in Google Compute Engine?

A. To create and manage virtual machines.

B. To define a set of rules for firewall configurations.

C. To manage and scale virtual machine instances efficiently.

D. To optimize content delivery through a Content Delivery Network (CDN).

Correct Answer: C

Explanation:

Instance groups in Google Compute Engine are used to manage and scale virtual machine instances efficiently, providing high availability and reliability.

Q No. 11 What is the primary advantage of using Google Cloud Storage as a storage option in Google Compute Engine?

A. It provides scalable and durable object storage.

B. It allows for the creation of virtual machine instances.

C. It facilitates secure access to instances using OS Login.

D. It automates the creation of instance templates.

Correct Answer: A

Explanation:

Google Cloud Storage is chosen as a storage option in Google Compute Engine primarily for its scalable and durable object storage capabilities.

Q No. 12: How does Cloud Armor contribute to security on Google Cloud?

A. By optimizing content delivery through a Content Delivery Network (CDN).

B. By providing fully managed file storage services.

C. By protecting applications and services from Distributed Denial of Service (DDoS) attacks.

D. By creating and running serverless functions that respond to events.

Correct Answer: C

Explanation:

Cloud Armor in Google Cloud contributes to security by protecting applications and services from Distributed Denial of Service (DDoS) attacks.

Q No. 13: What is the role of Cloud Router in Google Cloud networking?

A. To optimize content delivery through a Content Delivery Network (CDN).

B. To facilitate dynamic exchange of routes between on-premises networks and Google Cloud VPCs.

C. To manage permissions for service accounts.

D. To provide scalable and durable object storage.

Correct Answer: B

Explanation:

Cloud Router facilitates the dynamic exchange of routes between on-premises networks and Google Cloud VPCs, ensuring seamless connectivity.

Q No. 14: In the context of Google App Engine, what is the main differentiator between App Engine Flex and App Engine Standard?

A. App Engine Flex supports custom runtimes, while App Engine Standard supports only predefined runtimes.

B. App Engine Flex allows automatic scaling based on demand, while App Engine Standard provides manual scaling.

C. App Engine Flex is designed for stateless, serverless applications, while App Engine Standard is suitable for containerized applications.

D. App Engine Flex is fully managed, while App Engine Standard requires manual management of infrastructure.

Correct Answer: A

Explanation:

App Engine Flex supports custom runtimes, providing flexibility, while App Engine Standard is limited to predefined runtimes.

Q No. 15: How does Cloud Functions contribute to serverless computing in Google Cloud?

A. By creating and managing virtual machines.

B. By deploying and managing containerized applications.

C. By running lightweight, event-driven functions without the need for server management.

D. By providing fully managed file storage services.

Correct Answer: C

Explanation:

Cloud Functions in Google Cloud contributes to serverless computing by running lightweight, event-driven functions without the need for server management.

Q No. 16: What is the purpose of Cloud IAM in Google Cloud?

A. To create and manage virtual machines.

B. To manage permissions and control access to resources securely.

C. To optimize content delivery through a Content Delivery Network (CDN).

D. To facilitate dynamic exchange of routes between networks.

Correct Answer: B

Explanation:

Cloud IAM in Google Cloud is used to manage permissions and control access to resources securely within the cloud environment.

Q No. 17: How does Cloud Endpoints enhance API management in Google Cloud?

A. By providing scalable and durable object storage.

B. By optimizing content delivery through a Content Delivery Network (CDN).

C. By creating and running serverless functions that respond to events.

D. By enabling the creation, deployment, and management of APIs securely.

Correct Answer: D

Explanation:

Cloud Endpoints in Google Cloud enhances API management by enabling the creation, deployment, and management of APIs securely.

Q No. 18: What is the role of master nodes in Google Kubernetes Engine (GKE)?

A. To create and manage virtual machines.

B. To manage and orchestrate containers in the cluster.

C. To facilitate communication between nodes.

D. To provide scalable and durable object storage.

Correct Answer: B

Explanation:

In Google Kubernetes Engine (GKE), master nodes manage and orchestrate containers in the cluster, handling tasks such as scheduling and scaling.

Q No. 19: How does VPC Service Controls contribute to security in Google Cloud?

A. By optimizing content delivery through a Content Delivery Network (CDN).

B. By providing identity services, user management, and access control.

C. By facilitating dynamic exchange of routes between networks.

D. By enforcing additional controls over data access within Google Cloud services.

Correct Answer: D

Explanation:

VPC Service Controls in Google Cloud contributes to security by providing additional controls over data access within Google Cloud services.

Q No. 20: What is the primary advantage of using Google Cloud Load Balancing?

A. To optimize content delivery through a Content Delivery Network (CDN).

B. To distribute incoming traffic across multiple instances for optimal resource utilization.

C. To manage permissions and control access to resources securely.

D. To create and run serverless functions that respond to events.

Correct Answer: B

Explanation:

Google Cloud Load Balancing distributes incoming traffic across multiple instances for optimal resource utilization and application performance.

Chapter 8: Storage, Databases, and Data Analytics

This chapter explores the diverse storage, database, and data analytics services provided by Google Cloud. These services play a crucial role in managing and analyzing vast amounts of data efficiently and securely. Understanding the capabilities of Google Cloud Storage, databases like Cloud SQL, Cloud Spanner, and data analytics tools such as BigQuery and Cloud Dataflow is essential for designing scalable and performant applications.

Storage

Google Cloud Storage:

Delve into the capabilities of Google Cloud Storage, a scalable and durable object storage service. Learn about the different storage classes and access options for managing data in the cloud.

Cloud Filestore:

Explore Cloud Filestore, a fully managed file storage service, and understand how it provides high-performance, scalable file storage for applications running on Google Cloud.

Persistent Disk:

Understand the role of Persistent Disk in Google Cloud, providing reliable and high-performance block storage for virtual machine instances.

Local SSD:

Learn about Local SSD, a temporary, high-performance block storage option for virtual machine instances, suitable for temporary storage needs.

Databases

Cloud SQL:

Dive into Cloud SQL, Google Cloud's fully managed relational database service. Explore how Cloud SQL supports popular database engines like MySQL, PostgreSQL, and SQL Server.

Cloud Spanner:

Explore the globally distributed and horizontally scalable database service provided by Cloud Spanner. Understand its unique capabilities for handling globally distributed transactions.

Cloud Bigtable:

Learn about Cloud Bigtable, a fully managed, scalable NoSQL database service suitable for large analytical and operational workloads.

Cloud Firestore:

Explore Cloud Firestore, a serverless, NoSQL document database designed for web, mobile, and server applications, providing real-time updates and automatic scaling.

Cloud Memorystore:

Understand the managed, in-memory data store service provided by Cloud Memorystore, ideal for caching and speeding up the performance of applications.

Data Analytics

BigQuery:

Dive into BigQuery, Google Cloud's fully managed, serverless data warehouse. Explore its capabilities for fast SQL queries, real-time analytics, and seamless integration with various data sources.

Cloud Dataproc:

Learn about Cloud Dataproc, a fully managed and highly scalable Apache Spark and Hadoop service, facilitating the processing of large datasets.

Cloud Dataflow:

Explore Cloud Dataflow, a fully managed stream and batch processing service, enabling the development of data pipelines for real-time and batch processing scenarios.

Cloud Pub/Sub:

Understand Cloud Pub/Sub, Google Cloud's messaging service that enables event-driven computing, decoupling the senders and receivers of messages.

Data Security

Data Classification:

Explore data classification in Google Cloud, understanding how to categorize and label sensitive data to apply appropriate security measures.

Cloud DLP (Data Loss Prevention):

Learn about Cloud DLP, a service that helps discover, classify, and protect sensitive data using predefined and custom inspection rules.

Encryption:

Dive into encryption practices in Google Cloud, covering encryption at rest and in transit, and understanding how to leverage Google Cloud Key Management Service (KMS) for managing encryption keys securely.

Conclusion

This chapter has provided a comprehensive overview of Google Cloud's storage, databases, and data analytics services. From scalable object storage in Google Cloud Storage to fully managed databases like Cloud SQL and Cloud Spanner, and powerful data analytics tools such as BigQuery and Cloud Dataflow, you now have a foundational understanding of the services available for managing and analyzing data in the cloud.

Practice Exam Questions and Answers

Q No. 1: What is the primary purpose of Google Cloud Storage?

A. To create virtual machine instances.

B. To provide scalable and durable object storage.

C. To manage permissions and control access to resources securely.

D. To facilitate dynamic exchange of routes between on-premises networks and Google Cloud.

Correct Answer: B

Explanation:

Google Cloud Storage is designed to provide scalable and durable object storage in the cloud.

Q No. 2: What is the primary use case for Cloud Filestore?

A. To create and manage virtual machines.

B. To provide scalable and durable object storage.

C. To offer high-performance, scalable file storage for applications.

D. To facilitate the dynamic exchange of routes between networks.

Correct Answer: C

Explanation:

Cloud Filestore is used to provide high-performance, scalable file storage for applications running on Google Cloud.

Q No. 3: In Google Cloud, what is the purpose of Local SSD?

A. To provide scalable and durable object storage.

B. To offer high-performance, scalable file storage for applications.

C. To enable instances in a private subnet to access the internet while keeping source IP addresses hidden.

D. To provide temporary, high-performance block storage for virtual machine instances.

Correct Answer: D

Explanation:

Local SSD in Google Cloud provides temporary, high-performance block storage for virtual machine instances.

Q No. 4: Which Google Cloud service is fully managed and provides block storage for virtual machine instances?

A. Google Cloud Storage

B. Cloud Filestore

C. Persistent Disk

D. Local SSD

Correct Answer: C

Explanation:

Persistent Disk in Google Cloud provides reliable and high-performance block storage for virtual machine instances.

Q No. 5: What is Cloud SQL in Google Cloud?

A. A serverless, NoSQL document database.

B. A fully managed relational database service.

C. A globally distributed and horizontally scalable database service.

D. A managed, in-memory data store service.

Correct Answer: B

Explanation:

Cloud SQL in Google Cloud is a fully managed relational database service.

Q No. 6: In the context of databases, what is a key feature of Cloud Spanner?

A. Horizontal scaling for large analytical workloads.

B. Fully managed serverless architecture.

C. Globally distributed and horizontally scalable database.

D. A serverless, NoSQL document database.

Correct Answer: C

Explanation:

Cloud Spanner is a globally distributed and horizontally scalable database service.

Q No. 7: What is Cloud Bigtable in Google Cloud?

A. A fully managed relational database service.

B. A serverless, NoSQL document database.

C. A globally distributed and horizontally scalable database service.

D. A fully managed, scalable NoSQL database service.

Correct Answer: D

Explanation:

Cloud Bigtable is a fully managed, scalable NoSQL database service.

Q No. 8: What does Cloud Firestore offer in terms of database services?

A. A fully managed relational database service.

B. A globally distributed and horizontally scalable database service.

C. A serverless, NoSQL document database.

D. A managed, in-memory data store service.

Correct Answer: C

Explanation:

Cloud Firestore is a serverless, NoSQL document database designed for web, mobile, and server applications.

Q No. 9: What is the primary purpose of Cloud Memorystore?

A. To provide scalable and durable object storage.

B. To create and manage virtual machines.

C. To offer high-performance, scalable file storage for applications.

D. To provide a managed, in-memory data store service.

Correct Answer: D

Explanation:

Cloud Memorystore is designed to provide a managed, in-memory data store service.

Q No. 10: What is BigQuery in Google Cloud?

A. A globally distributed and horizontally scalable database service.

B. A serverless, NoSQL document database.

C. A fully managed, serverless data warehouse.

D. A fully managed relational database service.

Correct Answer: C

Explanation:

BigQuery is a fully managed, serverless data warehouse in Google Cloud.

Q No. 11: What is the primary use case for Cloud Dataproc?

A. Real-time analytics on large datasets.

B. High-performance file storage.

C. Fully managed serverless architecture.

D. Processing large datasets using Apache Spark and Hadoop.

Correct Answer: D

Explanation:

Cloud Dataproc is designed for processing large datasets using Apache Spark and Hadoop.

Q No. 12: What is Cloud Dataflow used for in Google Cloud?

A. Real-time analytics on large datasets.

B. Processing large datasets using Apache Spark and Hadoop.

C. Stream and batch processing for data pipelines.

D. A fully managed relational database service.

Correct Answer: C

Explanation:

Cloud Dataflow is used for stream and batch processing, allowing the development of data pipelines.

Q No. 13: What does Cloud Pub/Sub provide in Google Cloud?

A. A fully managed relational database service.

B. A serverless, NoSQL document database.

C. A messaging service for event-driven computing.

D. A globally distributed and horizontally scalable database service.

Correct Answer: C

Explanation:

Cloud Pub/Sub is a messaging service for event-driven computing in Google Cloud.

Q No. 14: What is the primary goal of data classification in Google Cloud?

A. To create and manage virtual machines.

B. To optimize content delivery through a Content Delivery Network (CDN).

C. To facilitate dynamic exchange of routes between on-premises networks and Google Cloud.

D. To categorize and label sensitive data for appropriate security measures.

Correct Answer: D

Explanation:

The primary goal of data classification is to categorize and label sensitive data for applying appropriate security measures.

Q No. 15: How does Cloud DLP contribute to data security in Google Cloud?

A. By optimizing content delivery through a Content Delivery Network (CDN).

B. By providing scalable and durable object storage.

C. By facilitating dynamic exchange of routes between networks.

D. By discovering, classifying, and protecting sensitive data using predefined and custom inspection rules.

Correct Answer: D

Explanation:

Cloud DLP contributes to data security by discovering, classifying, and protecting sensitive data using predefined and custom inspection rules.

Q No. 16: What is the purpose of encryption in Google Cloud?

A. To create and manage virtual machines.

B. To provide scalable and durable object storage.

C. To facilitate dynamic exchange of routes between networks.

D. To secure data at rest and in transit.

Correct Answer: D

Explanation:

Encryption in Google Cloud is used to secure data at rest and in transit.

Q No. 17: How does Cloud SQL enhance data security in Google Cloud?

A. By providing scalable and durable object storage.

B. By facilitating dynamic exchange of routes between networks.

C. By offering a fully managed, encrypted relational database service.

D. By creating and running serverless functions that respond to events.

Correct Answer: C

Explanation:

Cloud SQL enhances data security by offering a fully managed, encrypted relational database service.

Q No. 18: What is the significance of VPC Service Controls in Google Cloud?

A. By optimizing content delivery through a Content Delivery Network (CDN).

B. By providing identity services, user management, and access control.

C. By enabling instances in a private subnet to access the internet while keeping source IP addresses hidden.

D. By providing additional controls over data access within Google Cloud services.

Correct Answer: D

Explanation:

VPC Service Controls provide additional controls over data access within Google Cloud services, enhancing security.

Q No. 19: What is the primary advantage of using Google Cloud Load Balancing?

A. To optimize content delivery through a Content Delivery Network (CDN).

B. To distribute incoming traffic across multiple instances for optimal resource utilization.

C. To manage permissions and control access to resources securely.

D. To create and run serverless functions that respond to events.

Correct Answer: B

Explanation:

Google Cloud Load Balancing distributes incoming traffic across multiple instances for optimal resource utilization.

Q No. 20: How does Cloud Armor contribute to security on Google Cloud?

A. By optimizing content delivery through a Content Delivery Network (CDN).

B. By providing fully managed file storage services.

C. By protecting applications and services from Distributed Denial of Service (DDoS) attacks.

D. By creating and running serverless functions that respond to events.

Correct Answer: C

Explanation:

Cloud Armor contributes to security by protecting applications and services from Distributed Denial of Service (DDoS) attacks.

Chapter 9: Cloud Operations

In this chapter, we delve into the essential aspects of cloud operations on Google Cloud Platform (GCP). Cloud Operations involves managing and monitoring your applications and infrastructure to ensure they perform reliably and efficiently. We'll explore key tools and services such as Cloud Logging, Cloud Trace, Cloud Profiler, and Cloud Debugger, along with Cloud Monitoring, which is critical for maintaining the health and resilience of your cloud-based systems.

Cloud Logging

Log Types:

Understand the different types of logs generated by various GCP services. Explore how Cloud Logging provides centralized storage and analysis of these logs, offering insights into system behavior, performance, and security.

Cloud Trace, Cloud Profiler, and Cloud Debugger

Cloud Trace:

Explore how Cloud Trace helps you understand and optimize the performance of your applications by providing insights into latency and bottlenecks.

Cloud Profiler:

Learn about Cloud Profiler, a tool that helps you identify performance bottlenecks in your applications by capturing and analyzing CPU and memory usage.

Cloud Debugger:

Understand how Cloud Debugger enables you to inspect the state of your applications in real-time without affecting their performance, making it easier to identify and fix issues in production.

Cloud Monitoring

Workspaces:

Explore the concept of workspaces in Cloud Monitoring, providing isolated environments for managing monitoring configurations and data.

Monitoring Agent:

Learn about the Monitoring Agent, a tool that collects system and application metrics from your virtual machine instances, enhancing the monitoring capabilities of Cloud Monitoring.

Uptime Checks:

Understand the importance of uptime checks in Cloud Monitoring, enabling you to monitor the availability of your applications and services from various locations around the world.

Metrics and Alerts:

Dive into the world of metrics and alerts, exploring how Cloud Monitoring allows you to define custom metrics, set thresholds, and receive alerts to proactively respond to issues.

Dashboards:

Learn how to create and customize dashboards in Cloud Monitoring, providing a centralized view of the key performance indicators and metrics relevant to your applications.

The Importance of Resilience

Understanding Resilience:

Explore the concept of resilience in cloud operations, emphasizing the importance of designing systems that can adapt, recover, and thrive in the face of challenges.

Best Practices for Resilience:

Learn about best practices for building resilient applications, including strategies for fault tolerance, redundancy, and disaster recovery.

Incident Response and Post-Mortems:

Understand the importance of incident response and post-mortems in cloud operations, allowing you to learn from incidents and continuously improve your systems.

From logging and monitoring to tools like Cloud Trace, Cloud Profiler, and Cloud Debugger, you now have the knowledge and tools to ensure the reliability and performance of your cloud-based applications. The emphasis on resilience and best practices sets the stage for creating robust and adaptive systems in the dynamic cloud environment.

Practice Exam Questions and Answers

Q No. 1: What is the primary purpose of Cloud Logging in Google Cloud Platform?

A. To create and manage virtual machines.

B. To monitor and analyze logs generated by various GCP services.

C. To optimize content delivery through a Content Delivery Network (CDN).

D. To provide scalable and durable object storage.

Correct Answer: B

Explanation:

Cloud Logging is designed to monitor and analyze logs generated by various GCP services, offering centralized storage and insights into system behavior.

Q No. 2: What does Cloud Trace help you optimize in your applications?

A. Latency and bottlenecks.

B. CPU and memory usage.

C. File storage performance.

D. Uptime and availability.

Correct Answer: A

Explanation:

Cloud Trace helps you optimize the latency and identify bottlenecks in your applications.

Q No. 3: How does Cloud Profiler assist in application performance optimization?

A. By providing insights into latency and bottlenecks.

B. By capturing and analyzing CPU and memory usage.

C. By inspecting the state of applications in real-time.

D. By monitoring and analyzing logs.

Correct Answer: B

Explanation:

Cloud Profiler assists in application performance optimization by capturing and analyzing CPU and memory usage.

Q No. 4: What is the purpose of Cloud Debugger in Google Cloud?

A. To monitor and analyze logs.

B. To capture and analyze CPU and memory usage.

C. To inspect the state of applications in real-time without affecting performance.

D. To facilitate dynamic exchange of routes between networks.

Correct Answer: C

Explanation:

Cloud Debugger allows you to inspect the state of applications in real-time without affecting their performance.

Q No. 5: What is the primary function of a workspace in Cloud Monitoring?

A. To create and manage virtual machines.

B. To monitor and analyze logs.

C. To provide isolated environments for managing monitoring configurations and data.

D. To distribute incoming traffic across multiple instances.

Correct Answer: C

Explanation:

A workspace in Cloud Monitoring provides isolated environments for managing monitoring configurations and data.

Q No. 6: What does the Monitoring Agent do in Google Cloud?

A. It captures and analyzes CPU and memory usage.

B. It monitors and analyzes logs.

C. It enables instances in a private subnet to access the internet while keeping source IP addresses hidden.

D. It collects system and application metrics from virtual machine instances.

Correct Answer: D

Explanation:

The Monitoring Agent collects system and application metrics from virtual machine instances in Google Cloud.

Q No. 7: What is the significance of uptime checks in Cloud Monitoring?

A. To monitor and analyze logs.

B. To enable instances in a private subnet to access the internet securely.

C. To monitor the availability of applications and services from various locations.

D. To distribute incoming traffic across multiple instances.

Correct Answer: C

Explanation:

Uptime checks in Cloud Monitoring are significant for monitoring the availability of applications and services from various locations.

Q No. 8: How does Cloud Monitoring use metrics and alerts to proactively respond to issues?

A. By optimizing content delivery through a Content Delivery Network (CDN).

B. By defining custom metrics and setting thresholds for alerts.

C. By providing insights into latency and bottlenecks.

D. By capturing and analyzing CPU and memory usage.

Correct Answer: B

Explanation:

Cloud Monitoring uses metrics and alerts by defining custom metrics and setting thresholds to proactively respond to issues.

Q No. 9: What is the primary purpose of dashboards in Cloud Monitoring?

A. To monitor and analyze logs.

B. To distribute incoming traffic across multiple instances.

C. To provide isolated environments for managing monitoring configurations and data.

D. To create a centralized view of key performance indicators and metrics.

Correct Answer: D

Explanation:

Dashboards in Cloud Monitoring are used to create a centralized view of key performance indicators and metrics.

Q No. 10: Why is resilience important in the context of cloud operations?

A. To monitor and analyze logs.

B. To optimize content delivery through a Content Delivery Network (CDN).

C. To create and manage virtual machines.

D. To design systems that can adapt, recover, and thrive in the face of challenges.

Correct Answer: D

Explanation:

Resilience is important in cloud operations to design systems that can adapt, recover, and thrive in the face of challenges.

Q No. 11: What is a key strategy for achieving resilience in cloud applications?

A. Optimizing content delivery through a Content Delivery Network (CDN).

B. Fault tolerance, redundancy, and disaster recovery.

C. Creating and managing virtual machines.

D. Monitoring and analyzing logs.

Correct Answer: B

Explanation:

A key strategy for achieving resilience in cloud applications involves implementing fault tolerance, redundancy, and disaster recovery measures.

Q No. 12: Why is incident response important in cloud operations?

A. To distribute incoming traffic across multiple instances.

B. To optimize content delivery through a Content Delivery Network (CDN).

C. To enable instances in a private subnet to access the internet securely.

D. To learn from incidents and continuously improve systems.

Correct Answer: D

Explanation:

Incident response is important in cloud operations to learn from incidents and continuously improve systems.

Q No. 13: What is the purpose of post-mortems in cloud operations?

A. To optimize content delivery through a Content Delivery Network (CDN).

B. To create and manage virtual machines.

C. To monitor and analyze logs.

D. To analyze and learn from incidents that occurred.

Correct Answer: D

Explanation:

Post-mortems in cloud operations are conducted to analyze and learn from incidents that occurred.

Q No. 14: How does Cloud Monitoring contribute to the proactive management of cloud resources?

A. By optimizing content delivery through a Content Delivery Network (CDN).

B. By providing insights into latency and bottlenecks.

C. By collecting and analyzing metrics to monitor resource health.

D. By capturing and analyzing CPU and memory usage.

Correct Answer: C

Explanation:

Cloud Monitoring contributes to the proactive management of cloud resources by collecting and analyzing metrics to monitor resource health.

Q No. 15: What is the primary goal of Cloud DLP (Data Loss Prevention) in Google Cloud?

A. To create and manage virtual machines.

B. To optimize content delivery through a Content Delivery Network (CDN).

C. To facilitate dynamic exchange of routes between networks.

D. To discover, classify, and protect sensitive data.

Correct Answer: D

Explanation:

The primary goal of Cloud DLP is to discover, classify, and protect sensitive data in Google Cloud.

Q No. 16: How does encryption contribute to data security in Google Cloud?

A. By providing scalable and durable object storage.

B. By optimizing content delivery through a Content Delivery Network (CDN).

C. By facilitating dynamic exchange of routes between networks.

D. By securing data at rest and in transit.

Correct Answer: D

Explanation:

Encryption in Google Cloud contributes to data security by securing data at rest and in transit.

Q No. 17: What is the role of Cloud SQL in enhancing data security in Google Cloud?

A. By providing scalable and durable object storage.

B. By optimizing content delivery through a Content Delivery Network (CDN).

C. By offering a fully managed, encrypted relational database service.

D. By capturing and analyzing CPU and memory usage.

Correct Answer: C

Explanation:

Cloud SQL enhances data security in Google Cloud by offering a fully managed, encrypted relational database service.

Q No. 18: How does VPC Service Controls enhance security in Google Cloud?

A. By optimizing content delivery through a Content Delivery Network (CDN).

B. By providing identity services, user management, and access control.

C. By facilitating dynamic exchange of routes between networks.

D. By capturing and analyzing CPU and memory usage.

Correct Answer: B

Explanation:

VPC Service Controls enhance security in Google Cloud by providing identity services, user management, and access control.

Q No. 19: What is the primary advantage of using Google Cloud Load Balancing?

A. To optimize content delivery through a Content Delivery Network (CDN).

B. To distribute incoming traffic across multiple instances for optimal resource utilization.

C. To monitor and analyze logs.

D. To create and run serverless functions that respond to events.

Correct Answer: B

Explanation:

The primary advantage of using Google Cloud Load Balancing is to distribute incoming traffic across multiple instances for optimal resource utilization.

Q No. 20: How does Cloud Armor contribute to security on Google Cloud?

A. By optimizing content delivery through a Content Delivery Network (CDN).

B. By providing fully managed file storage services.

C. By protecting applications and services from Distributed Denial of Service (DDoS) attacks.

D. By creating and running serverless functions that respond to events.

Correct Answer: C

Explanation:

Cloud Armor contributes to security on Google Cloud by protecting applications and services from Distributed Denial of Service (DDoS) attacks.

Conclusion

Congratulations on completing this comprehensive guide designed to help you prepare for the Google Certified Professional Cloud Architect certification exam. Throughout this book, we've explored the key concepts, services, and best practices necessary to succeed in the role of a Cloud Architect on the Google Cloud Platform (GCP).

Your Journey to Google Cloud Expertise

As you've navigated through the chapters, you've gained insights into:

Cloud Computing Fundamentals: Understanding the core principles of cloud computing and how Google Cloud differentiates itself in the cloud services landscape.

Google Cloud Services Overview: Exploring a broad spectrum of GCP services, from computing and storage to databases, networking, and security solutions.

Identity and Access Management: Managing cloud identities securely and implementing access controls using Cloud IAM.

Resource Management: Effectively organizing resources using the Cloud Resource Manager and implementing organization policies.

Networking Deep Dive: Understanding the intricacies of Google's global network, Virtual Private Clouds, subnetting, and various networking security features.

Compute and Containers: Working with Google Compute Engine, Google App Engine, Google Kubernetes Engine, Cloud Functions, and other related services for application deployment and management.

Storage, Databases, and Data Analytics: Exploring Google Cloud Storage, Cloud SQL, Cloud Spanner, Cloud Bigtable, BigQuery, and other services for managing and analyzing data.

Cloud Operations: Monitoring, logging, and optimizing performance with tools like Cloud Logging, Cloud Trace, Cloud Profiler, and Cloud Debugger.

Practice Exams and Test Preparation

To solidify your knowledge, we've provided a set of practice exam questions and detailed explanations. These questions mimic the format and content you may encounter in the actual certification exam. Regularly practicing these questions will help reinforce your understanding and improve your confidence.

Conclusion: Your Next Steps

As you conclude this learning journey, here are recommended next steps:

Hands-on Practice: Apply your knowledge by working on real-world projects and experimenting with GCP services. The more hands-on experience you gain, the more confident you'll become.

Review and Reinforce: Revisit the chapters and practice questions periodically to reinforce your understanding and stay up-to-date with any changes in GCP services.

Join the GCP Community: Engage with the Google Cloud community, forums, and events. Networking with other professionals can provide valuable insights and support.

Stay Informed: Cloud technology evolves rapidly. Stay informed about updates, new features, and best practices by following GCP documentation, blogs, and official announcements.

Schedule Your Exam: When you feel ready, schedule your Google Certified Professional Cloud Architect exam. Use the knowledge and skills you've acquired to confidently tackle the exam questions.

Best of Luck!

Embarking on the journey to becoming a Google Certified Professional Cloud Architect is a commendable endeavor. Your commitment to learning and mastering cloud technologies positions you for success in architecting robust and scalable solutions on Google Cloud Platform.

Wishing you the best of luck in your certification journey and in all your future endeavors in the dynamic and exciting field of cloud computing! Before you go, I kindly ask you to write a review for this book, as it will help me improve my writing style and skills for my future books.

If you enjoyed this book, then I would like to ask you for a small favour. Would you be kind enough to leave an honest review for this book?

I'd much appreciate it.

www.ingramcontent.com/pod-product-compliance
Lightning Source LLC
LaVergne TN
LVHW082351200926
848481LV00012B/3535
9798223071914